#Twitterbook

How to Really Use Twitter

Andreas Ramos

andreas.com

About this Book

#TwitterBook was first published in October 2013, updated in October 2014, and updated again in March 2019. ISBN 9781798575994

See andreas.com/book-twitterbook.html

About the Author

Andreas has written fourteen books about digital marketing and SEO. He teaches digital marketing at INSEEC SF, AcademyX, and CSTU. Andreas has worked at SGI, SUN, and more than 25 Silicon Valley startups. He was the Manager of Global SEO at Cisco. He co-founded two digital marketing agencies and is on the advisory board of nine startups. He lives in Palo Alto with his wife and cat.

Visit him at andreas.com or on Twitter at @andreas_ramos

Technical Editor

#TwitterBook was reviewed by Monte Clark @monteclark who found many errors and often, found better tools.

Acknowledgements

Many thanks for valuable suggestions from Lt. Chris Hsiung (Palo Alto Police), Lt. Zach Perron (Mountain View Police), and Anaximander Katzenjammer (office cat). Cover design by Ginger Namgostar.

Trademarks

Names of companies and products in this document are trademarks, registered trademarks, or trade names of their respective holders, and have been used in an editorial fashion only.

Dedication

For Gong Zhihong

Table of Contents

If you read only three chapters, read chapter 3, *How to Tweet*, chapter 6, *Search*, and chapter 11, *Twitter in a Disaster*.

Chapter 1. Quick Setup: Set up your account. Multiple accounts. Page 9

Chapter 2. Followers: Who to follow, fake followers. Page 17

Chapter 3. How to Tweet: #Hashtags, Tweets, Photos, Video, Polls, Pins, Threads, Moments, Dashboards, Competitors, Mentions, Mute. Page 24

Chapter 4. Twitter Lists: How to find, read, and create. Page 43

Chapter 5. Who Uses Twitter? A few notes about a few people on Twitter. Page 51

Chapter 6. Search and Twitter: Use Twitter to research and find jobs. A note on SEO. Page 62

Chapter 7. Ads in Twitter: How to use ads in Twitter. Page 65

Chapter 8. Analytics in Twitter: Page 67

Chapter 9. Twitter after Dark: Sex, Drugs, and Loud Music. Revolution, censorship, tracking, harassment. Page 70

Chapter 10. Police and Twitter: How the police use Twitter. Page 78

Chapter 11. Twitter in a Disaster: When the lights go out. Page 84

Examples: Sample Twitter plans for a play and a conference, plus a strategy for setting up and managing Twitter. Page 83

Closing: Why use Twitter. Page 89

References, Resources, Glossary, and Index: Page 90

#TwitterBook by @Andreas_Ramos

Why I Wrote This Book

In summer 2013, the *New Yorker* wrote an article about Steubenville, a small town in Appalachia. There are few jobs, little education, and not much to do. In passing, the article mentioned how people in that town, including high school kids, moms, teachers, bloggers, cops, and lawyers used Twitter and YouTube. I saw people in Appalachia used social media better than we did in Silicon Valley.

I began talking with friends in Silicon Valley: engineers, marketing people, directors, founders, investors, and so on. I kept hearing the same thing over and over: "I don't get Twitter."

- The head of a social media company with several million dollars in venture capital funding confided to me he didn't get Twitter

- A marketing expert had sent several thousand tweets to 40,000 followers over four years said to me, "I use it because everyone else uses it, but I don't get it."

- The CMO of a global corporation asked me, "What is this Twitter? My kids keep talking about it."

Here's the best story. In mid-2008, I spoke at a conference at UC Berkeley. The speaker after me was Biz Stone, one of the founders of Twitter, to talk about Twitter. Someone asked him why their company should use it. He shrugged and said, "I don't really know." Not even Twitter got it.

I signed up for Twitter a few days later to see what he was talking about. I'll admit, it took me a while to figure it out.

In writing this book, I talked with a lot of people and looked at hundreds of Twitter accounts of marketing people, engineers, kids, rappers, and moms. I look at accounts in the USA, Mexico, Colombia, Brazil, Denmark, Sweden, Norway, Finland, France, Germany, and other countries. I got to the point that I can glance at someone's account and tell if they get it or not. After you read this book, you can do the same.

How this Book Is Different

Nearly every FAQ, blog, or book about Twitter was written by marketing people who want you to be their client so they won't tell you bad stuff about Twitter or social media.

I don't want to sell you anything. Really. I want to show you how Twitter works so you can use it for yourself and your company.

How Did Twitter Start?

In early 2006, a small team of engineers were working at a startup in San Francisco. After discussing various ideas, they put together a messaging tool. It took off at South by Southwest (a sort of startup event).

Twitter had eight years of endless rounds of funding, internal fistfights, lack of innovation, and several founders got thrown out. Some of the founders won't even talk to each other. *Hatching Twitter* by Nick Bilton (2013) is an appalling description of how the company was built.

Difference between Facebook and Twitter

Most people understand Facebook, so let's compare the two:

- Facebook is like a party in your backyard. You invite 100 friends and family. When you talk, only those around you can hear you, not the entire party, not the neighborhood, not the city. You can't post a message to Facebook that can be seen by two billion people. When you post on Facebook to your friends, Facebook shows your message to only about 15% of your friends.

- Twitter is like the Egyptian revolution. Everyone mills around in chaos. Every posting goes out to all sides: friends, enemies, demonstrators, the government, the army, journalists, and the rest of the world.

So, Just Exactly What Is Twitter?

What is Twitter? Why do people use it? What's the power of Twitter?

Twitter is microblogging for mobile devices. Any tweet can be seen by everyone. You can see what anyone is saying. You can follow any topic. You can contact anyone.

What about Other Social Media Sites?

I manage digital marketing for a billion-dollar global organization. The web analytics shows me that traffic comes from 61 social media sites. Which one is the best?

Use your analytics to see which sites produce the best results for you. Don't use something just because it's what you know, it's popular, or someone recommended it.

Different Uses of Twitter

People use Twitter in several different ways:

- **Celebrities** broadcast to their followers
- **Marketing** broadcasts about their products and services
- **Journalists** follow news, look for sources, research, and look for people to interview
- **People Find out** about companies, products, and services
- **Jobs** are posted to Twitter and jobseekers find those jobs
- **Topics** are discussed by people
- **Researchers** in STEM (science, technology, engineering, medicine) plus other academic fields, including professors and graduate students use Twitter to share research, discuss, and keep up

If you're a celebrity or a marketer, contact Twitter at dev.twitter.com. They have all sorts of teams to help you. You can also try Twitter Advertising.

What's with the Bird?

Figure 1: Larry Bird, the logo of Twitter. The guys who came up with Twitter thought the short messages were like chirps, so it's called Twitter and tweets. The Twitter bird's name is Larry Bird, possibly named after a US basketball player from the 80s. Twitter paid Simon Oxley, a British graphics designer, $15 for the logo. Simon also designed Octocat, the GitHub logo.

Why Is this Book Exactly 100 Pages Long?

This book is actually only 86 pages, but Amazon won't allow me to publish a book with only 86 pages. It must be 100 pages. I had to add a few extra page breaks, a few extra paragraphs, and a bit of blank space to stretch it to one hundred pages.

But don't worry. You're paying for 86 pages and you get 100 pages!

Closing Summary

Twitter is a place for global discussion where you can contact anyone on Twitter. No other social media platform offers that.

Chapter 1: Setting Up Twitter

In this chapter, I'll quickly cover the basics of Twitter. It'll be short because it's easy to set up Twitter.

If you've already set up Twitter, skim this or skip the chapter.

Setting Up Your Twitter Account

There are several settings that you can change in your account:

- **Change Your ID**: One of the nice things is that you can change your ID whenever you like. In college, you were @WildDawg but you're now a lawyer in Washington, D.C., so you can change your Twitter ID to @GoeffreyThrockmortonIII.

- **Add a Short Bio**: You have room for a short description under your photo. People can use search engines and find this, so use keywords and hashtags, plus your city and URL.

- **Set Your Photo**: Your photo tells people a great deal about you. If you're in the professional class, use your logo or a professional portrait. If you're using Twitter for personal reasons, use a casual snapshot. You can also use a selfie, your dog, Bugs Bunny, your boobs, or whatever. It depends on how you want others to see you. For best results, use a 73x73 photo.

- **Change the Profile Photo and Background Photo**: You can also change the background. There are two backgrounds: the one behind your photo and the one behind your tweets. Go to my Twitter page. See the books at the top? That's the background. To change that, go to your Twitter page. Click your photo at the left. At the right side, a "Edit Profile" button appears. This lets you change the header photo (the background) and the profile photo (photo of you). To make a background photo, search for "how to change background on Twitter." There are plenty of guides to this. Why do this? An account with a professional background looks better.

- **Clean Up Your Past**: If you're looking for a job or a date, you may want to clean up your tweets. For better or worse, employers, girlfriends, and others may look at the ghost of your past. Many companies use software to collect all of your social postings. You may want to erase irrelevant or embarrassing tweets.

More about the Short Bio

Here's a bit more about your short profile description. Under your photo, you can add a short description. For several years, it was popular to use this as a mini-resume along with personal statements, such as "Loves Italian food and puppies."

However, some people use tools such as FollowerWonk to look for contacts in Twitter. You should write your profile to enable tools to find you.

- You have 160 characters (including spaces)

- Add a three- or four-word description of what you do (plus hashtags) and where you work

- Add your city and website or blog

- Make sure you show up in FollowerWonk, Twellow, and TwtrLand. Go to those sites and register your profile.

Here is my Twitter bio: Author of 14 books on #SEO (4 #1 Amazon Best Sellers) | Instructor of Digital Marketing at INSEEC SF & CSTU | Startup Advisor | Universität Heidelberg

Use your Twitter ID

Make it easy for people to contact you in Twitter. Put your Twitter ID in your email signature, webpage, Facebook profile, PowerPoint presentations, business card, and so on.

More Settings

You can do several things in your Twitter settings:

- Connect your Twitter account to your cell phone. Go to Settings | Mobile and add your cell phone. Turn on Direct messages. To prevent messages at 3 a.m., turn on the Sleep Settings.

- If you want your cell phone to notify you when someone sends you a direct message (DM), turn on cell phone notification for Direct Messages. Go to Settings | Mobile, enter your cell phone number, and select "Direct Messages."

- You can allow anyone to contact you (or block that). Turn this on at Settings | Privacy and Settings. Checkmark "Direct Messagese".

- Many apps and sites will request access to your Twitter account. Some will steal your personal information. Every once in a while, I delete whatever I'm not using. Go to Settings | Apps and Devices and click Revoke Access.

There are many more settings. Go through these and see which ones are useful for you.

Set Twitter to Private

Anything you post in Twitter can be read by anyone anywhere in the world. To keep it private, set your account to Private.

Private groups can be useful for work teams, role playing games, school groups, groups of friends, families, and so on.

To set your account to private, click Settings | Security and Privacy | Protect my Tweets. If someone wants to follow you, they apply and you can accept or reject them.

About 8% of accounts are set to private.

Set Up Multiple Accounts

Facebook wants you to have only one account, but Twitter doesn't mind if you set up several accounts. There are several good reasons to do this:

- In an organization, staff can have their own accounts along with an account for the organization, each division, each product, and so on. A team can share the ID and password for organization accounts so they can post to it.

- Public and personal accounts. Teens use a public account for parents and a private account for their friends.

There are also bad reasons to set up fake accounts:

- People create fake conversations. They say something and then use other accounts to support or attack themselves. Whenever you see someone take a socially dangerous position, such as calling for peace, twenty others will attack him. Those twenty people may be the same person. These are called sock puppets, as in people who use hand puppets to argue with themselves.

- Be careful in online magazines and forums. Political groups and governments often use sock puppets to attack people. Many rabid postings to progressive, pacifist, or liberal magazines are fake. If you suggest it may not be nice to bomb a baby whale, 500 people will attack you relentlessly. These are fake accounts from an oil company. The accounts have photos, bios, tweets, and followers. It's all fake.

- Many advertising and marketing agencies also create fake accounts so they can show their clients how much the public loves the product.

Verified Accounts

There are also Verified Accounts. A small blue checkmark shows up next to the name, which means that's the person's real account. For example, see @Greenpeace.

Be careful when you follow your favorite celebrity. There are dozens of fake accounts for celebrities. Some are quite convincing. Look for the verified account.

Twitter does this for people in music, movies, fashion, government, politics, religion, journalism, media, business, and so on. They also verify some companies. This is a we'll-call-you kind of thing. If you have lots of followers, Twitter may contact you.

Take Over an ID

Many accounts are created and abandoned. If you want a Twitter ID but someone else has it, look at their tweets. If they haven't tweeted in six months, the account may be abandoned.

Twitter sees no reason to protect inactive accounts. If you can show why you should have that ID, they may turn it over to you. I've done this several times for clients.

If you have a trademark on your name (for example, Samsung) but someone is using the name, contact Twitter. Show proof of your trademark and Twitter will turn the account over to you.

Lost Your Access?

Okay, your CEO let a hottie intern set up the company Twitter account and now she went elephant trekking in Burma. You don't know the password for the account.

If you can prove who you are, Twitter will change the password. I've done this for several clients. But this isn't easy. It took months to recover an account for an airline. Don't let interns set up accounts.

Add a Twitter Feed to Your Webpage

You can place a small window on your webpage (or blog) with a feed from your Twitter account. This can show your tweets or tweets about a topic. This is easy to do. Just copy and paste a few lines of code to embed a Twitter box.

Go to https://publish.twitter.com/# and follow the instructions.

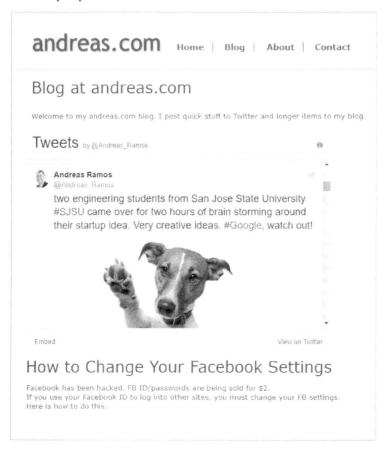

Figure 2: At my website's blog page, I added a Twitter feed. You can easily add a Twitter feed to your website or blog. Just copy/paste a few lines of code.

How to Use Several Twitter Accounts

You can have several accounts: one for personal, another for business, and so on. Each product, division, or department in your organization can have an account.

It's easy to switch from one account to another:

- In Android, click your photo at the top left of the page. Click the tiny down-arrow. You can create a new account. You can switch to another account.

- In Apple, go to your profile. Click the more-icon (the three little dots). You can create a new account or switch to another account.

This works only in mobile Twitter, not in desktop Twitter.

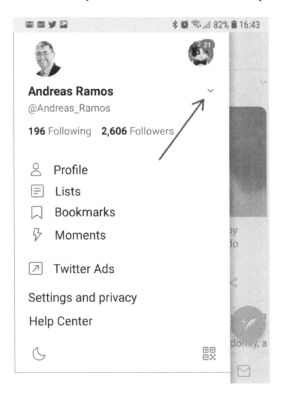

Figure 3: In Android, click the little down arrow to switch between accounts.

Who Owns Your Account, Anyway?

Who owns your account? If your intern gets 300,000 followers, what happens when she leaves? If you spent a great deal of money to make her popular and she leaves, they'll often go with her. That's happened with several social media people.

Use your organization's name in the Twitter ID and make it clear to staff that the organization owns the account. Use an organization email address for the account's access so you can recover or change the password.

Closing Summary

See? Other books cover setup in a hundred pages, but I did it in three pages. That's the easy stuff. Next is followers and hashtags.

Chapter 2: Followers

Let's look at followers in Twitter.

What's the Story with Followers?

One of the ways to measure success is to look for numbers. When you have a lot of bottle caps, you're the king of bottle caps on your street. Of course, that starts the race to collect bottle caps every way you can.

The same on Twitter. Twitter shows you how many people follow you which turns into a game for the sake of numbers.

It's understandable to want followers. It's sad to tweet if nobody is listening. It's cool to see your follower numbers go up.

And that's okay for most people, but two groups go too far: celebrities and bean counters. A celebrity's weight is measured in fans. 10 million fans are bigger than 4 million. Celebrity magazines love these lists.

Bean counters have 500 fans which is nowhere near celebrity status, so they'll do anything to get more fans.

Celebrities, movie stars, musicians, politicians, and many more have fake followers. For example, a Hollywood celebrity has 20 million followers in her Twitter page. You look closely and you wonder if they're real or fake. You can use StatusPeople.com to see that five million (25%) of her followers are fake. Another five million followers are inactive accounts. Only ten million (50%) are real accounts.

Or are those really real? The best bot companies can create fake followers with full profiles and a history of comments. They copy the online behavior of millions of people which they use to simulate behavior so the bots act like people. How many of her ten million real accounts are actual people? It's impossible to tell.

If an account has fake followers, it doesn't mean the person bought fake followers. Anyone can buy fake follower for any account.

There are tools such as Manageflitter to remove fake or inactive followers. However, in early 2019, Twitter turned off their API access.

You don't need 100,000 followers. You can have only two followers (your mom and your cat) and that's okay, because if you use good hashtags, people can find your postings. It's the content that matters, not the number of followers.

How to Find People to Follow

Follow the top people in your field. They talk about what they do.

- Use hashtags to find the discussions you want to follow

- Use other tools that find the key people in a field. In most fields, this is okay; people generally don't inflate their numbers. However, if fields include celebrities, sports, politics, movies, TV, marketing, advertising, or sales, many of those people will use tricks to increase their numbers.

Here are some of the tools that I use to find people:

Figure 4: **FollowerWonk** lets you find people and sort them by the number of tweets, how many they follow, how many follow them, and social authority (a score). But again, be careful: it's easy to fake the numbers.

If you use a good tool, let me know.

Who to Follow

Look for relevant postings by people who use Twitter to talk with other people. You want people who engage in conversations, not just broadcast. There are three criteria for true experts:

- Credentials: They have certificates from leading authoritative institutions which have a strict selection process, such as graduation from MIT

- Expertise: They are experts at what they do and they are acknowledged by other experts. They are cited by other experts in published materials.

- Experience: They have substantial experience (ten years or more) in their field

Look for leading technical experts, university professors, or academic researchers in your field. You can also look for authors of the top books in your field. See if they are in Twitter and if they maintain a list (there's a chapter in this book about Twitter Lists).

This doesn't mean experts are only Stanford and MIT graduates. Many fields aren't defined by universities. For example, Tony Hawk is the world's leading expert on skateboards, Stephanie Gilmore is a world-class surfer, and Serena Williams is an expert in tennis. For non-academic fields, look for authors who've been published by leading publishers or magazines.

However, there is so much confusion, much of which has been created by social media influencers. These people use Twitter to inflate their appearance. Regrettably, social media allows braggarts, clowns, and extremists of all kinds to make an impact. The more provocative they are, the more followers they get. This doesn't make them experts.

How to Get Fake Followers

There are several ways to get followers:

- Buy followers. Pay $10 for 1,000 followers. Use a search engine and look for *buy Twitter followers*. Many organizations, movie stars, and politicians use this to get 3,000,000 followers (you can get a bulk discount for 100,000 or more). You can buy fake followers for Facebook, Instagram, YouTube, and just about every social site.

- Create followers. Companies will create fake accounts that you can manage. A director at a global marketing company told me they have an army of zombie accounts which they use to add fake Likes, Followers, and comments to their clients. Clients get happy when they see 300,000 followers cheering the dumb product. (Several people asked me about this so-called global marketing company. On advice from an attorney (really), I can't say the name because they may sue, regardless of the facts.)

Another Way to Get Followers

There's another way. Many people will follow you if you follow them.

- Follow 300 people on Monday. Just pick them at random. Go to someone's page (especially someone with lots of followers) and look at their list of followers. Do clicky-clicky and add people at random.

- About 150 of them (50%) will follow you in return

- On Tuesday, follow another 300 people. You'll get another 150 followers.

- Keep doing this. You can add 150 followers every day. After 30 days, you'll have 4,500 followers.

- Keep doing this. You can easily get 20-30,000 followers.

Like I said, this works, and I know because I tested it for you, my dear reader.

Figure 5: My cat created a Twitter account with a photo, bio, and two tweets about Lady Gaga. Every day, my cat followed 100 people. When he had followed 1,000 people, 552 (55%) followed my cat in return. You can do this to get 4,500-5,000 followers in a few weeks.

- Search Twitter for #followback to find people who'll follow you if you follow them. 70% or more will follow you.

- Don't add more than 300-400 people per day. Twitter doesn't like aggressive following. They'll pause or delete your account.

You don't have to find random people. Use FollowerWonk or similar and find people in your field with many followers. Go to their account and look at following/followers. When you see profiles that look good, follow them. Follow one hundred people every day. Some people do this and get 20% to follow them in return. There are tools such as ManageFlitter to remove the ones who don't follow you.

#FF Follow Friday

#FF is short for *Follow Friday*, a tradition on Twitter. On Fridays, some people will post lots of tweets with names of others to follow. They're saying, "hey, here are some more people for you to follow." For example: #FF @monteclark @rachelstone @JoJo @Miffy @catherine @Ilya

This is like #Caturday, when people post cat pictures on Twitter. Whatever.

What's the Point of Fake Followers?

There are several useful reasons to get fake followers:

- A friend, who is a journalist at a large nationwide newspaper, called me one day. His editor saw that he had only 300 followers and said, "Bob, that doesn't look too good." He has a wife, two kids, and a house and was terrified that he would get fired. I told him how to buy fake followers. The other journalists had about 10,000 followers, so he bought enough to be in line with them.

- The same has happened to friends who work in social media at companies: if they can't get the numbers up, they get replaced, so they buy followers.

- In your Twitter profile, Twitter recommends several people for you to follow. Why are they chosen to be shown to you? Because they have lots of followers. If you have only two followers, you won't be recommended to others, so you won't get more followers. If you have 900 followers or more, you'll be recommended to others. The more you get, the more you'll be recommended so it starts to grow faster.

- Celebrities must appear to be popular so their press agents add a few million followers. The followers are happy to feel they're following a leader.

- Customers often choose a product based on social numbers. If your product has 300 followers and your competitors have 10,000 followers, it may hurt your sales. Buy enough followers to be slightly ahead of your competitors.

Be careful. When you buy followers, you may be dealing with hackers who create fake accounts to infect computers. That leads to credit card fraud, bank fraud, and blackmail. If you buy fake followers, use a debit card that doesn't have your name.

This is also why I think most social metrics tools are worthless because they can be easily spoofed. Want a big social authority score? No problem! Whip out your credit card and you'll be a local hero.

As you'll see in the next chapter on hashtags, the number of followers doesn't matter. It's not followers that matter. It's the discussions.

Get Real Followers

There's another way to get followers:

- To see which of your friends are on Twitter, go to your Twitter account. At the far right, there is "Who To Follow" box. At the bottom, click on "Find people you know". Twitter will show you which of your friends have Twitter accounts. Follow them. Ask them to follow you.

- Add your @name to your email address line, your website's contact page, and your pages at Facebook, LinkedIn, and so on

- Write useful articles, blogs, newsletters, and books

- Talk at conferences and put your Twitter ID in your presentations

Does Twitter Care about Fake Followers?

A group of researchers were able to find several million fake accounts which Twitter then deleted. See the *Resources* section for more information.

But there are many more fake accounts. Twitter could easily get rid of those fake and inactive accounts, but that would lower the number of Twitter accounts by 20-30% and the stock would fall, so Twitter does nothing about this.

Closing Summary

This chapter covered the basics of followers and following. Ready for the good stuff? The next chapter covers tweets and hashtags.

Chapter 3: How to Tweet

Twitter is all about hashtags, not followers. What matters is talking with other people about something, which happens with hashtags. Let's look at hashtags.

A Quick History of #Hashtags

Hashtags started on IRC (a chat group on the Internet) in the late 1980s. In 2007, twenty years later, people began to use them on Twitter. At first, Twitter tried to ignore them ("looks too techie"), but after a few years, millions of people were using them, so in 2010, Twitter began indexing them. Yep, Twitter ignored hashtags for three years. See? Not even Twitter got it.

By spring 2013, six years after hashtags started in Twitter and twenty-five years after hashtags started on IRC, the highly innovative teams at Facebook and Google invented them.

This wasn't Twitter's only mistake. They didn't invent @replies or retweets either. Users came up with that. For several years, the founders of Twitter didn't understand why anyone would do this. They didn't (and some still don't) realize that people use Twitter for conversation.

What Are #Hashtags?

First of all, these are called hash tags, not pound tags. Hashtags aren't technical things like links or meta tags. They're just ordinary words with a hash mark (#) in front of them.

By adding the hash mark, you mark the word, like using underline or bold. You use it to tell other people that the word is important.

Twitter made the hashtags clickable. When you see a hashtag, you click it and Twitter will show you more tweets with that hashtag. It's the same as if you search for it. You'll see all of the postings with that hashtag. This lets you follow the conversation and add to it.

For example, to see what people are saying about Miley Cyrus, search for #MileyCyrus. (By the way, upper case or lower case doesn't matter, so you can use #MileyCyrus, #mileycyrus, #MiLeYcYrUs, or whatever.) Hashtags are written as one word. It's #MileyCyrus, not #Miley Cyrus.

First, be sure that you're using the right hashtag. A number of organizations have tried to invent their hashtags, but for whatever reason, the community chose a different hashtag. Use hashtag tools to see what's being used. For example, you can see that one hashtag has been used twenty times in the last thirty days, but another hashtag has been used 35,000 times.

When you've settled on the hashtag, use it in your tweets. Put it in your webpages, website, emails, newsletters, business cards, advertising, T-shirts, TV ads, and digital advertising. Use it in your Google Adwords, both text ads and banner ads. Use it in Facebook, Instagram, and other social platforms.

Who Owns a #Hashtag?

There's no registration or ownership of a hashtag. Anyone can use it.

According to US copyright law, you can't copyright a word or title. You may be able to trademark a hashtag, but it would be difficult to keep others from using it.

Twitter shows only recent tweets. Nobody looks at tweets more than a few months old. This means a hashtag that was in use two years ago but has been abandoned can be used for a different purpose today.

The best way to assert control over your hashtag is to register it at the hashtag definition sites and use it regularly.

Hashtags, Discussions, Communities

In the beginning, the idea for social media sites such as LinkedIn and Facebook was networks of small groups of friends. This was based on research by Mark Granovetter, dean of sociology at Stanford, and others. Social communication happened within small groups of people.

But Twitter allows your posting to be seen by anyone. Absolutely anyone. To most people, this is a bloomin' buzzin' confusion of tweets about celebrities, personal chit-chat, and some dog's lunch, which is many people look at Twitter and never come back. Many keep using it but never figure out what's going on.

To solve that mess, people began using hashtags. With search and hashtags, you suddenly see only the tweets for that topic.

- Want to see what's going on in NYC? Search for #NYCEvents. 227 tweets in the last 30 days.

- What have people said about sushi in Seattle? Search #Seattle #Sushi. 35 in the last 30 days.

- Wondering about that beach at Maui? #beach #maui. 587 tweets in the last 30 days, many with photos.

- Earthquake in Sichuan? Get instant updates with #earthquake #Sichuan.

- What's going on at Oracle World conference? Go #OracleWorld

- Is the SF commuter train late? #Caltrain for updates.

- What's the latest about Kim? #KimKardashian

- Looking for a job in sales in Paris? Search #sales #job #Paris. 24 openings in the last 30 days.

US political groups use hashtags so their conversations can be seen by their members. There is #TCOT (Top Conservatives on Twitter), #TDOT (Top Democrats on Twitter), #CCOT (Conservative Christians on Twitter), and so on. They stay in touch and talk with each other by using hashtags.

Hashtags come and go. Some stay in use for a long time. Others pop up, become wildly popular, and disappear within a few days. Look around and see what's being used.

Tools to Find #Hashtags

Here are several useful tools to find hashtags:

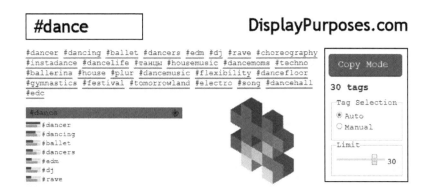

Figure 6: At DisplayPurposes.com, you enter a #hashtag and it shows a list of related #hashtags, sorted by use. It's easy to copy the list to add to your tweet.

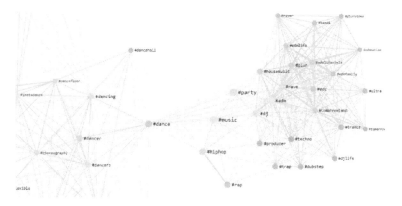

DisplayPurposes also shows you tweets as clusters. The illustration shows #dance is used by two groups: ballet and rave parties, so you have to be careful to use the right #hashtags.

DisplayPurposes also lets you see the popular tweets in any city.

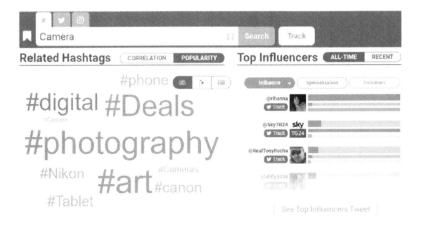

Figure 7: **RiteTag** shows #hashtags, the top people, their tweets, and sentiment. People are ranked by their relevance, including the number of their followers who are also relevant to the discussion.

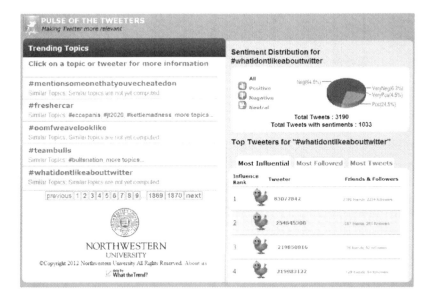

Figure 8: **PulseOfTheTweeters.com** shows #hashtags, the top people, their tweets, and sentiment. People are ranked by their relevance, including the number of their followers who are also relevant to the discussion.

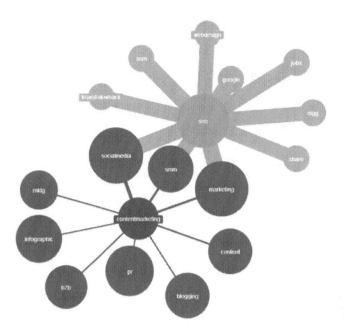

Figure 9: **Hashtagify.me** shows you related #hashtags. What's the best one for helicopters? #helicopter, #copter, or #whirlybird? Enter #helicopter, and see related #hashtags. You'll see a word that I didn't include in my list. The size of the circle shows popularity; the thickness of the line shows traffic; and the closer the circle, the more relevant.

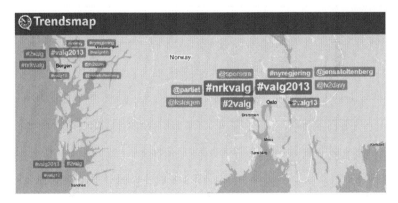

Figure 10: **TrendsMap.com** lets see current hashtags worldwide by city, county, and region. In the illustration, you can see lots of attention for elections in Norway.

If you find other useful tools, let me know!

Which #Hashtag Tool to Use?

I use all three: DisplayPurposes.com, RiteTag.com, and Hashtagify.me. They give slightly different results. Pick the best hashtags.

What to Tweet

Many of the experts in your field are on Twitter. You can learn more about your field. Ask questions:

- Ask about products, tools, and services
- Ask about organizations, conferences, and events
- Ask for the best books, websites, blogs, and other resources
- Ask for ideas to improve your product
- Talk about tips, ideas, observations, discoveries

Look at their tweets to see the hashtags that they use.

How to Write Tweets

It's not about you :-(Show what your reader can learn from you.

- Talk in your own voice, as you talk with your friends
- Talk about your work and your life
- Don't broadcast at people. Ask questions. Use polls.
- Post three to five times every day

Use Text, #Hashtags, Links, Photos, and Video

A tweet is more than text.

- Add a hashtag so others can find your tweets
- Add links, photos, and videos

Eye tracking studies show that people read the first few words of a tweet to see if it's interesting. Put your main idea at the beginning. Don't write, "If you're looking for a nice restaurant in Tokyo for tacos from Pakistan…" Write, "#Pakistani #tacos in #Tokyo at #Jimmy's #TacoPalace."

Hashtags in Other Social Sites

Facebook and Google added hashtags, but few people use them. That's not surprising. When you use Facebook, you're not posting to all two billion Facebook users. Facebook is a private garden party where you post to only your friends.

Instagram, Pinterest, and others also use hashtags.

Use Memes, Photos and Video in Twitter

A meme or photo gets attention. A video gets yet more attention.

You can get free stock photographs at Pexels, PixaBay, Burst, Crello, DepositPhotos, Gratisography, Kaboom, PicJumbo, PikWizard, StockSnap.io, and Unsplash.

Use Polls in Twitter

Let your audience vote on questions.

Figure 11: Use polls to interact with your audience. Ask them serious questions or silly questions. To do this, ask a question. At the bottom, click the "**poll**" symbol. You can add choices. You can also set the time for the poll, such as 24 or 48 hours.

Pin a Tweet

You can pick a tweet to always appear at the top of your page. This will be the first tweet that people read when they visit your site. You can change this whenever you like.

Figure 12: Pin a tweet to the top of your page. To do this, go to your account, select a tweet, click the little arrow, select "Pin to your profile page". You can also write a tweet with information, links, hashtags, and a favorite photo to use as the pinned tweet.

Use Threads to Post a Series of Tweets

Sometimes, a 280-character tweet isn't enough. You can write a thread of up to ten tweets.

Figure 13: Use Thread to write a series of tweets. Start the first tweet. At the bottom of the tweet, click the plus-sign. Write the second tweet. Use the plus-sign to add more tweets. You can also add photos and polls.

Twitter Moments

Twitter Moments is another way to present a series of tweets. With Threads, you show a series of your own tweets. With Moments, you can collect a series of tweets such as events, conferences, products, and so on by other people (your team, the audience) and show the tweets, photos, video, and so on as a series.

If your Moment is about hiking, then people who read tweets about hiking or follow hikers may see your Moment in their list of Moments.

If your Moment gets enough traffic or it's a popular topic, it may show up in Twitter's Moments page. Most Moments are written by Twitter's team. Moments are seen by about 100m people every month, which is more than The New York Times, The Washington Post, and CNN combined. Why so many? Because it's in Twitter and news media don't have social platforms.

This new dog museum is all about man's best friend

TicToc by Bloomberg ● 1 hour ago

Figure 14: Use Moments to present a set of tweets. To create Moments, use Twitter on desktop (not on mobile). For details on how to create Moments, see help.twitter.com/en/search?q=how+to+create+a+moment

Tips for Tweeting

Hire some staff to send your tweets. That's how @MileyCyrus tweets every 42 seconds all day (and all night too.) Celebrities have a staff of two or three people to tweet. Companies often have several people as well. Cisco has more than 100 Twitter accounts.

You can use the schedule tools in HootSuite and TweetDeck to write ten or twenty tweets at once and then send them out over the week.

Hootsuite and TweetDeck also have team management tools, so your team can write tweets in draft mode and submit them to you for approval and release.

RT Retweets

If someone reposts your tweet to her followers, that's a *retweet* (often abbreviated as RT).

You can also ask people to retweet your message. At the end of your tweet, add Please Retweet! (or just Pls RT) and people will pass it along.

But retweets metrics are easy to fake. Buy 10,000 fake accounts, post a tweet, and have your 10,000 zombies retweet it.

Look at your Competitors

Find three-to-five relevant people or organizations in Twitter. For example, to find to find French banks in Twitter, use Google to search <site:twitter.com banque france>. Follow them. Every quarter, review their pages. Write a short summary of each page:

- What's their goal?
- Number of Likes/Followers: Good, bad, and why?
- Banner photo: Good or bad, and why?
- Profile pictures: Good or bad, and why?
- Postings: Good or bad, and why?
- Ratio of postings: Text, photo, and video
- How often do they post?
- What are they talking about?

Tweetchats

A tweetchat is an online live discussion around a topic. Someone uses a hashtag to announce a tweetchat on a topic for a day and time, such as Thursday 9 a.m. Paris. Everyone can join the chat by using the hashtag. People can ask questions or add comments by using the hashtag.

When you have sufficient audience around a topic, you can set up a tweetchat. It can be on a weekly schedule or it can be spontaneous.

To hold a 30-minute tweetchat, write perhaps five questions. Announce the start of the event and state the first question, for example, "Q1 What do you think of my last video?" Let people reply. When things slow down, post Q2. Ask questions to get the audience to reply. You can reply or comment to their replies.

You can do this even if you only have a few followers. Look for a discussion with a large active audience (say, 5,000 tweets with that hashtag in the last 30 days) and announce your tweetchat.

To find tweetchats, search for #tweetchat, ask leading people, or go to TweetChat.com, which has a calendar of dozens of topics with hundreds of chats. For example, within the education category, there's #MDChat for doctors (Tuesdays, 9 am EST).

Bored celebrities sitting at the airport may suddenly announce to their two million followers that they have a free hour: what do they want to know? Fans love this sudden access. If you're managing tweets for a celebrity but he's up on the roof, trying to catch his pet iguana, just announce that he's available and start tweeting for him.

See What Someone Likes to Tweet About

Do you want to see what someone is tweeting? Create a word cloud of her tweets and you'll see what's important for her.

Figure 15: Use a word cloud to see at a glance someone's interests. Here's a word cloud for my tweets. You can see I'm writing about Twitter, startups, poetry, books, advertising, and Google.

How to Make a Tweet Cloud

You can make a tweet cloud in a few steps:

- Go to anyone's Twitter page
- Scroll down perhaps six months or get a few hundred tweets
- Use Control+A to select all and copy the tweets
- Go to WordArt.com, click Words, and then Import
- The tweets turn into a word cloud

Twitter should add a word cloud button so you can quickly evaluate someone's tweets.

Contact People with @messages

One of the cool things about Twitter is the open network. You can contact anyone on Twitter. Just write a tweet and include their @name. For example, to contact Emmanuel Macron, president of France, send a tweet that includes @EmmanuelMacron. His team will see it.

This makes it easy to reach experts and authors. Put their Twitter name in your tweet and they will see your message and they may reply.

The Difference between @reply and @mention

There's a different in how you write a message with a @name. It's either a reply or a mention.

Let's say you want to talk with Laura (and let's say she uses @Laura at Twitter):

- If you start a tweet with @Laura, then that's a @reply. It's a semi-private message that will be seen by only by you, Laura, your followers, and Laura's followers. Your tweet won't be available to the rest of the world. For example, "@laura how about lunch today?"

- If you put @Laura inside the tweet, then it's called a @mention. It's a public message and anyone can see it. For example, "how about lunch in Seattle today @laura"

- You can add a period at the beginning of the tweet (just before the @Laura) to convert an @reply into an @mention, which turns it into a public tweet. For example, ".@laura how about lunch in Seattle today?" (Note the period before the "@")

Here's a non-technical explanation. Okay, you're at dinner with a group of friends. You say, "Laura, can you pass me the salad?" You're asking Laura, but everyone else can hear it. But if you say, "The salad was made by Laura," then you're talking to everyone.

Send a Direct Message (DM)

You can also send a tweet as a private message, but it depends on the recipient.

- If both of you follow each other, you can send direct messages

- If she doesn't follow you, but she set up her account to allow direct messages from people she doesn't follow, she'll get your message

- If she doesn't follow you and she didn't turn on direct messages from everyone, she won't get your message

How to Track Tweets

You can track tweets in your web analytics. Do this by using tracking URLs and analytics. That gets a bit complicated and I wrote about it in *The Big Book of Content Marketing* (#BBoCM) so I won't cover it here.

Hashtag Hijacking

Before I close this chapter, a short note about hashtag hijacking. Some people use hashtags to jump into unrelated discussions.

For example, people are talking about #Greenpeace and #whales. Someone wants to sell junk pills, so he'll send a bunch of tweets that include #Greenpeace, #whales, and offers for pills. He's spamming the conversation among Greenpeace users.

Regrettably, many marketers are doing this. If there's a hashtag with lots of traffic, they try to see how they can offer their products. Marketers and spammers are using hashtags during disasters and sports events to flood the conversation with their offers.

Don't do this. It annoys people and they'll click the spam button or report you for abuse. Twitter may shut down your account.

Use Mute, not Block

Some people complain about anything. Don't block them. They'll only get angry and attack more. Instead of Block, use the Mute option. You won't see their postings and they won't know you don't see their postings.

Figure 16: Use Mute to get rid of critics. Go to the person's posting, click the little arrow, select "Mute @accountname".

Dashboards for Twitter

It's much easier to use Twitter with a dashboard. A dashboard is a collection of columns where you use each column to show tweets for a topic. One column shows the tweets that you follow. Several columns show the tweets for hashtags that you follow, such as your company, product, and so on. Another column can show all tweets by one person. Dashboards make it much easier to use social media.

Figure 17: **Hootsuite** lets me follow hashtags. There's a column for each hashtag, such as #PaloAlto and #OnlyInSiliconValley. I follow a few hashtags, plus conferences and events which I add or remove as they come and go.

You can set up columns for your organization, your products, and services. You can follow people, topics, or lists. You can follow your school, your sports team, or your town.

The dashboards also let you send tweets, schedule tweets for later posting, search, and so on. You can also manage tweets as a team: someone on your team writes a tweet and it goes to you for approval. These dashboards also let you add postings from Facebook, LinkedIn, and other social sites.

If you're using Twitter for work, it's a good idea to put this on a separate screen so you can watch the columns. You can set up bell notifications to get your attention or just bug your co-workers.

Dashboards include Tweetdeck (owned by Twitter), Hootsuite, and others. TweetDeck is very good on desktop, but there isn't a mobile version. The Hootsuite app is good for mobile.

How to Download Your Tweets

Do you want to see every tweet you've ever posted? Or you want a copy, just in case? You can get a copy of your tweets. It's also a good way to see your first tweet so you know when you joined.

To do this: Go to your Twitter page. Click your profile icon at the upper right. In the drop-down menu, select Settings and privacy. At the bottom, Request Your Archive.

Closing Summary

Twitter is about topics and hashtags, not followers. Search topics and hashtags to participate or read conversations.

Chapter 4: Twitter Lists

When someone finds a group of people who tweet about a topic, he can create a Twitter List. That's a list of those people.

If you're interested in a topic, you can find the Twitter lists for that topic and read their tweets.

You subscribe to the collection, not the person, so they won't know that you're following them.

You can also create your own list, both public (to share) and private (only for you.

This chapter will show you:

- How to find lists in Twitter
- How to read lists in Twitter

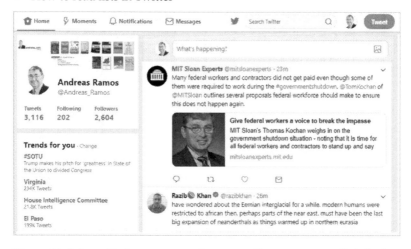

Figure 18: Select a Twitter account. Go to your Twitter account (I clicked on my account @andreas_ramos). Click on someone who you follow, such as @MITSloanExperts.

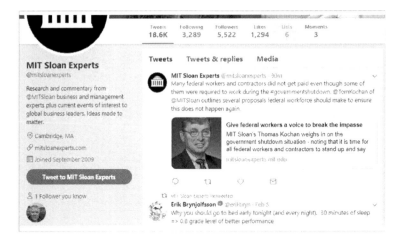

Figure 19: On the page for MITSloanExperts, click the link at the top for Lists. Some people don't have any lists (either they don't know or they don't bother).

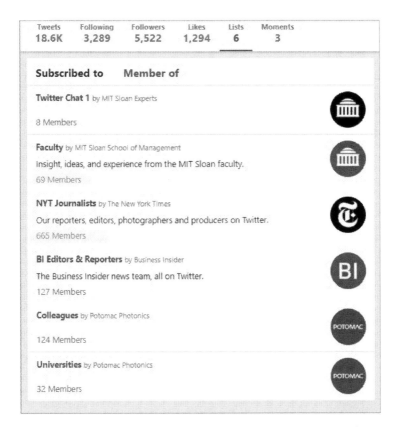

Tweets	Following	Followers	Likes	Lists	Moments
18.6K	3,289	5,522	1,294	6	3

Subscribed to   **Member of**

Twitter Chat 1 by MIT Sloan Experts

8 Members

Faculty by MIT Sloan School of Management

Insight, ideas, and experience from the MIT Sloan faculty.

69 Members

NYT Journalists by The New York Times

Our reporters, editors, photographers and producers on Twitter.

665 Members

BI Editors & Reporters by Business Insider

The Business Insider news team, all on Twitter.

127 Members

Colleagues by Potomac Photonics

124 Members

Universities by Potomac Photonics

32 Members

Figure 20: You can then see the lists to which @MITSloanExperts has subscribed. For example, the list NYT Journalists has 665 members. The list Faculty is professors at MIT (69 members). Let's see that list. Click on Faculty.

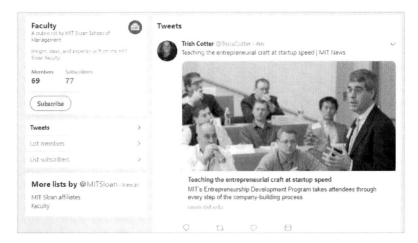

Figure 21: We can see what members are posting in that list. If we like it, we can subscribe to the list by clicking "Subscribe".

Figure 22: To read your lists, go to your Twitter account and click the link for Lists.

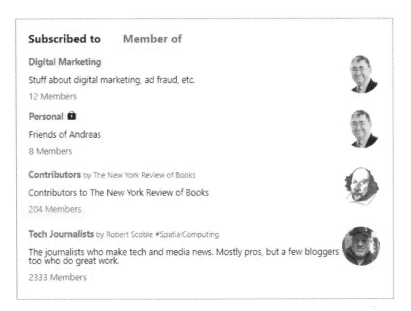

Figure 23: It shows you the lists to which you've subscribed. Let's read the Contributors list, so click Contributors.

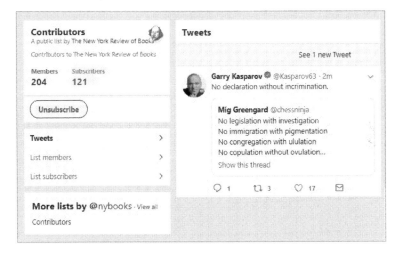

Figure 24: The list appears and you can read the most recent postings. If you don't like the list, you can quit by clicking "Unsubscribe".

Tip: It's easier to read the lists to which you've subscribed by using Hootsuite. Instead of adding Twitter account, you can add a list to which you've subscribed. It appears in your Hootsuite screen. Just swipe sideways to go through each list.

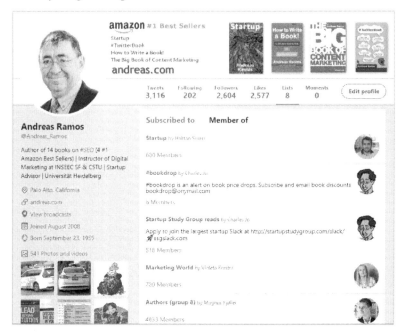

Figure 25: See if you're a member of a list. People can also add your account to their lists. This means there may be Twitter lists out there that show your tweets. Go to your account. Click Lists. In the new box, click "Member of".

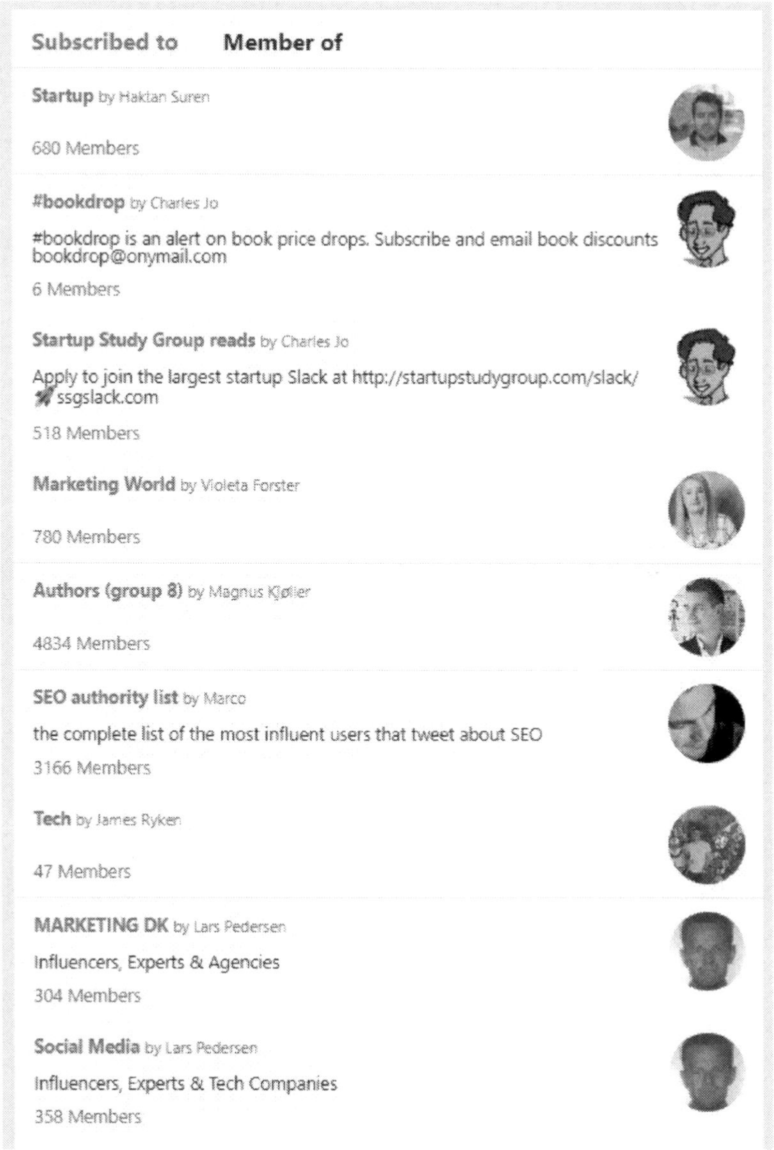

Subscribed to	Member of

Startup by Haktan Suren

680 Members

#bookdrop by Charles Jo

#bookdrop is an alert on book price drops. Subscribe and email book discounts bookdrop@onymail.com

6 Members

Startup Study Group reads by Charles Jo

Apply to join the largest startup Slack at http://startupstudygroup.com/slack/ ssgslack.com

518 Members

Marketing World by Violeta Forster

780 Members

Authors (group 8) by Magnus Kjøller

4834 Members

SEO authority list by Marco

the complete list of the most influent users that tweet about SEO

3166 Members

Tech by James Ryken

47 Members

MARKETING DK by Lars Pedersen

Influencers, Experts & Agencies

304 Members

Social Media by Lars Pedersen

Influencers, Experts & Tech Companies

358 Members

Figure 26: See the Lists that Show Your Tweets. This shows you the lists to which people have added you. I've been added to 85 lists, which are read by some 83,850 people.

But that doesn't mean they are actually reading my tweets. It's up to each person to open the list and read it.

It isn't always good to be on a list. Some people get added to lists of idiots and so on.

If you've been added to a list where you don't want to be, you can block the person who created the list

There doesn't seem to be a way to find out if your name has been added to a list. If you know how to do this, let me know and I'll update this.

You can also create private lists, for example, friends, family, co-workers. Create the list and select Private. This can be useful to follow your company, school, and so on.

Make a List

It's easy to make a list for any topic. FollowerWonk shows you the people who use keywords in their profile (if they haven't registered at FollowerWonk, they won't be included).

- Go to FollowerWonk and search for variations of the keyword, such as evolution, evolution theory, evolutionary biology, evolutionarybiology, and so on

- Sort by number of followers, copy the top 50, and paste into a text file

- Sort by number of tweets, copy the top 50, and paste into a text file

- Use the text editor to delete everything but the tweeter IDs

- Create a list and add the names

- As you read the new list, you can delete whomever is posting irrelevant stuff

Summary

If you're interested in a topic, someone may have made a list for it. You can also create lists of people so you can keep up with a topic.

Chapter 5: Who Uses Twitter?

Who Uses Twitter?

Who is on Twitter? What are they doing? Is there any way to get an overview of Twitter or it is the world's biggest chatroom?

Let's Go to the Numbers

One way is to look at the number of categories. Twellow sorted discussions into 2,750 categories. TwtrLand lists 2,027 topics and 60,000 skills. So Twitter isn't just about @MileyCyrus.

Another way is to look at the people who use Twitter. (The data in this section comes from the Pew Study on US teens. See References for a link.)

- 16% of adults who use the web also use Twitter

- 95% of teens use the web

- 77% of teens use Facebook

- In 2009, 8% of teens (age 13-19) used Twitter

- In 2011, 12% of teenagers used Twitter

- In 2013, 24% (7.2m) of teens were using Twitter

- 10.8m adults age 18-29 (27% of all adults) use Twitter

Only 16% of adults (40m) use Twitter, but 24% of teens (7.2m) use Twitter. An additional 10.8m young adults (18-29) are on Twitter.

Teens are increasingly using Twitter, where they're catching up to young adults. Twitter is becoming a teenage space. It's interesting that everyone thinks teens are the early adopters of communications and social media, but it was adults who were the early adopters and after seven years, teens finally got aboard.

Teens aren't abandoning Facebook. Pew writes there is no evidence of a mass exodus from Facebook. However, Facebook's Likes, commenting, and tagging creates social tension for teens. Teens feel they must be on Facebook so they don't miss out, but they're adding other tools, such as Twitter and Instagram (11% use Instagram in 2013, vs. none in 2012), so they can communicate in other ways. Only 1% of teens use Gmail (7% user Tumblr; 3% use Google+).

There are differences by race:

- 19% of US Latino teens are on Twitter

- 23% of US white teens are on Twitter

- 39% of US black teens are on Twitter

Nearly 40% of black teens are on Twitter. As we know, US black teens create many cultural trends, which include clothes, music, and dance. White teens often copy black teens. Justin Bieber started as a Christian gospel singer and Miley Cyrus started as Hanna Montana, the Disney child star, but both adopted black music to further their careers.

- Boys and girls 12- and 13-years old behave the same. But the 14-17 age group is three times more likely to use Twitter than younger children. Girls 14 to 17 are twice as likely to use Twitter as boys in the same age group. There's no difference by household income. Rich and poor teens use Twitter equally.

- Teens tend to maintain smaller circles in Twitter. The median (typical) teen has 300 friends in Facebook but only 79 in Twitter. 24% of teens have set their Twitter account to private so only their approved friends can see tweets (in contrast, 60% of teens have set their Facebook account to private.)

- Finally, for whatever reason, many teens say "a Facebook," as in "I asked my mom for a Facebook" or "I have a Facebook."

For data, see the Pew Report *Teens, Social Media, and Privacy* in References.

Is This Good for Twitter?

If you look at Twitter's FAQs, there's not a word about black teens or teens in general. Social sites want lots of members, but there's such a thing as wrong members. I worked on a project with a major social media company. For whatever reason, their site became very popular in another country. They had over 10m teenage girls. However, US advertisers wanted to advertise to US adults. They had no interest in advertising to teenage girls in another country.

Let's see what teens are doing.

Black Twitter

There are so many black teens on Twitter that they've created their own world on Twitter. People talk about "Black Twitter". These kids have come up with new ways to use Twitter.

Use TrendsMap to look at trending hashtags. First of all, tweets tend to concentrate around large cities. Hashtags spring up suddenly, grow explosively, and disappear within a few days.

Many of these are by and for black teens. They write "fill in the blank" tweets, such as #IfSantaWasBlack or #InPhilly (you know you're in Philadelphia if…) The replies are witty and often very funny. Paula Deen got her own #PaulasBestDishes hashtag. Go ahead and look up some of these hashtags.

I think this comes out of *Call-and-Response*, a tradition in US Black culture. You've seen this in movies that include Black churches, where the preacher calls out to the audience and they shout back a reply and it goes back and forth. For whites, it's disruptive, but some blacks like it that way.

Several factors come together:

- US Blacks and Latinos are early adopters of mobile devices, with Latinos leading whites as much as three to one for smart phones.

- Blacks and Latinos tend to have strong family networks and they stay in touch with each other. Latino families may also live in several countries. So they use phones to stay in touch.

- US urban Blacks and Latinos teens can use Twitter on $5 cell phones.

Look at several hundred tweets by black teens and you'll see they nearly always use hashtags, photos, and videos. They tweet in group conversations by sharing their thoughts and experiences. This is in contrast to celebrities who use Twitter for one-way broadcast.

Black teens are also using Twitter to meet new people. The Pew study points out 54% of black teens have become good friends with people they've met online in comparison to 35% of white teens.

This brings me back to what I wrote at the opening of this book. I noticed people in Appalachia knew Twitter better than people in Silicon Valley. Looking at Twitter, I found widespread underground use. Black teens didn't read books on how to use Twitter; they figured this out on their own and the remaining teens joined them.

Look at people's tweets. If it's a long series of "official tweets" with capitalized words and URLs to articles, then the person is broadcasting. He's not listening. Is the person a "Like Whore" collecting followers for the sake of numbers? Ask them, and I've found out that if they know you well enough, some will admit they don't get Twitter.

Latinos on Twitter

There are 542 million people in Latin America and another 52 million Latinos in the USA. If we assume the common 16%, adoption rate, that's 95m Latinos on Twitter, or about twice as many as Americans on Twitter.

That's why many of the top hashtags are in Spanish, such as #TodoIbaBienHastaQue (#EveryThingWasGoingWellUntil…) with very funny completions (these are all in Spanish).

Use TrendsMap to look at hashtags in South America and Central America.

Chinese on Twitter

It's hard to know how many Chinese use Twitter. Along with Twitter, Google, Facebook, and several other companies are blocked in mainland Chinese.

However, many Chinese use Virtual Private Networks (VPN) to connect to these sites. The VPN disguises the user's location, so someone in Beijing appears to be in Chicago and thus can use Twitter. This also means you don't know where the user is located, so it's difficult to know the number of Chinese on Twitter.

Figure 27: **WeChat** has over 900 million users. You can add photos, videos, and animated cartoon characters. I use WeChat more than SMS.

Chinese use WeChat in China instead of Twitter. WeChat has voice calling, video calling, group chat, animated emoji, news, local maps, and more. WeChat digital payment is connected to your credit card and bank account. Millions of Chinese companies have WeChat accounts so you can take the train to the airport, buy an airline ticket, take a taxi, go shopping, reserve a hotel room, and pay in a restaurant, all in WeChat. Nearly a billion people use one universal digital payment tool. This means future versions of social media will come from China. There's another thing about Wechat that's different from English. Chinese write in Chinese, which has a big impact on what you can say. A tweet allows 240 characters which allows you write a short message with about 24-40 English words (and lots of abbreviations and acronyms). But in Chinese, you can write a word with a single character. Chinese also uses fewer spaces between characters, so a tweet in Chinese can have 240-260 words. This allows six times more words than English, which also allows them to write longer, complex thoughts that are impossible to express in English in a short tweet. Ai Weiwei, the Chinese artist, said "With 280 Chinese characters on Twitter, you can write a short story or novel." Would you like an example? This paragraph has 240 words, which would fit in a Chinese tweet, but would be impossible to tweet in English.

TV on Twitter

Up until the mid-90s, people watched TV at home and talked about the show at the office or school the next day.

Now, those conversations occur during the show. Many people watch TV with their cell phones or tablets in hand and make comments via Twitter at the characters in the show, to the actors, and to each other. People also invent new characters and add dialog. It turns into chaos of comments and insults.

TV producers and Twitter realized audience participation was increasing attention, so they joined the riot. The TV show displays hashtags on screen. #MTVHottest was tweeted 166 million times in 90 days. Often, they release new hashtags after each commercial break to provoke uproar. Many TV actors have a team who tweet backstage during the show.

Social TV spread into sports, where games are accompanied by as many as 150,000 tweets per minute. 44% of Super Bowl ads have hashtags. Beyoncé's Super Bowl halftime show reached 268,000 tweets per minute.

Twitter encourages advertisers to participate. TV ads include hashtags so viewers can talk about the products or look for more information. Advertisers can also use Twitter Advertising to show ads in Twitter that appear only to people watching the show. Clever, no? TV in Twitter and Twitter in TV. Twitter bought Bluefin in early 2013 for $50m, which they can use to find the volume of tweets for a brand. This data allows Twitter to approach more companies for advertising.

However, there's a problem. Since anyone can use any hashtag, other advertisers can also add unpaid advertising to TV events. Don't have $3m for a Super Bowl ad? Use the hashtags for the game, the players, or official advertisers in your tweets and post messages. The audience will see them.

The TV team at Twitter has tips and ideas for media, TV, sports, journalism, celebrities, and similar. For more, see:

- @twittermedia (by Twitter)
- dev.twitter.com/media
- dev.twitter.com/media/twitter-tv

Web 1.0, Web 2.0, Social Media, and Engagement

The difference between Web 1.0 and social Web 2.0 is engagement. In Web 1.0, the owner created a webpage to broadcast his message at the audience. The audience's role was to buy. This meant traditional marketers measured results by sales and revenue. Since engagement can't show revenue or sales, they ignored that as a metric.

They're right, in a sense. There are very little sales in social. Many organizations have found they may have millions of Facebook Likes but very little revenue.

This underscores the difference between Web 1.0 and social. Social isn't a platform to broadcast messages or offer products at an audience. Social is a platform where people talk together:

- You identify your audience

- What are their interests and questions?

- You answer their questions

Engagement and Organizations

So if Twitter is about conversations, how does that work for business?

For decades, most organizations handled communication with their customers as a one-way street. Organizations talked at the customers. If customers talked back, that could be seen as feedback, which was sometimes used to improve services and products, but mostly, it was ignored. Most organizations didn't have a way for customers to talk with other customers.

Social media broke this model. First, customers can easily (and loudly) talk back at organizations. If customers use ridicule or satire, their message can spread further than the organization's marketing message.

The marketing communications department likes to manage the contact with customers to control the company message. But Twitter lets customers quickly find people within your organization and talk with them. People can see tweets by your staff, contractors, and suppliers. The woman in the cafeteria or the guy in security may be tweeting about the company.

Social also lets customers talk with each other. Organizations have no control over this, and if they try to control it, the backlash can be worse.

But organizations can't ignore social media. People will talk about them anyway. At best, the organization should participate in the conversation and try to steer it in a positive direction.

I use organization as the general concept for governments, public services, universities, churches, business, and club. All of these groups are learning to use social to talk with their communities.

What Does the Fox Say?

When Twitter IPOed (started selling stock in Wall Street), they had to file an S-1 document with the government. The S-1 stated they had 215m monthly active users (MAUs). On p. 46, they admitted there was no independent confirmation of this number (see http://1.usa.gov/16J0RMo, 233 pages, HTML).

Twitter counts the active accounts. This includes:

- Humans: A person logs into Twitter to read messages or send a message.

- Multiple accounts: Many people use several accounts. For example, someone may have two accounts for personal and work use. A company team may have 10-20 accounts for different purposes (an account for each product, each service, the company, the CEO, the company dog, and so on). Large corporations may have hundreds of accounts.

- Robots: Many computers log into Twitter to collect messages or send messages. For example, weather and earthquake reports are automatically sent.

- Automated activity: Your cell phone automatically checks Twitter every few minutes for new messages. Each of those automated checks is an activity. It's possible someone set up Twitter on her phone four years ago but forgot about it, yet she's still considered a daily active user.

- Spammers: Marketing and spammers create millions of fake accounts to send messages.

All of these are considered active accounts.

A better way is to see how many humans use Twitter. The *Pew Internet and American Life Project* (PewInternet.org) found 16% of US adults (20-75 years old) use Twitter. There are about 250m adults in the US, so that's 40m adult Americans on Twitter.

Pew also finds 24% of US teenagers use Twitter (May 2013). There are 30m US teenagers (age 13-19), many of whom had a party next door last night. So that's 7.2m teens on Twitter.

This means 47.2m people in the US on Twitter in mid-2013.

People at Twitter told me 77% of their users are outside the US. If 47.2m are in the US, then there are an additional 128m people outside the US for a total of 175m people. An additional 40 million accounts are multiple accounts, robot accounts, fake accounts, or spam accounts.

Mike Isaac at *AllThingsDigital* wrote Twitter has had over a billion registrations, which means the abandonment rate is greater than 83%.

Why do people sign up but not use Twitter? Twitter won't explain to people how to use it. The interface is also primitive and confusing. Furthermore, Twitter encourages Twitter a something for celebrities, so everyone else has little incentive to use it.

Twitter's visibility is greater than its use. TV shows, billboards, and advertising now show hashtags and tweets. A study by Edison Research and Arbitron shows that 44% of Americans see tweets daily through other media.

Be careful with data before 2012. In 2011, only 12% of teens used Twitter but in 2013, 26% of teens were on Twitter. These numbers can quickly change.

Researchers estimate 3% of accounts are fake (around 5 million accounts). Twitter themselves say about 5% (11m) are fake. (Yes, I've read estimates of 10-20%, but I think the lower numbers are better justified.)

There around 500m tweets per day, but many are automated or spam.

Documentation for these numbers is in the References section.

If you have a better way to calculate Twitter's numbers, please let me know.

Closing Summary

Twitter isn't just San Francisco hipsters. It's widely used by black teens, Latinos, along with people in practically every profession and skill. They use hashtags to find each other and talk.

Chapter 6: Search and Twitter

Let's look at how to find stuff in Twitter, how to use Twitter for research, and how to do SEO in Twitter.

Use Twitter Advanced Search

There's basic search via the Twitter search box. Twitter's Advanced Search is much better. Go to twitter.com/search-advanced to use it.

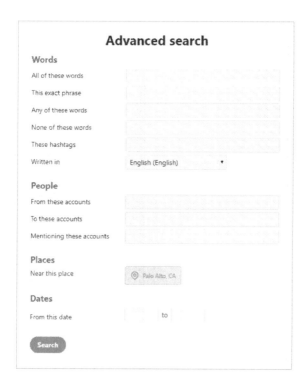

Figure 28: **Twitter Advanced Search** at twitter.com/search-advanced

The Advanced Search tool lets you search Twitter in several ways:

- Advanced Search lets you search keywords and hashtags. You can also exclude keywords. You can search in 51 languages.

- You can search for tweets from a person or to a person

- You can also search by location, such as your city

- You can use question marks to find tweets where people are asking questions

If you have a business, use this to find questions about your products or services. You can find potential customers, existing customers, and your competitors' customers., For example, if you sell traditional Arabic sushi in Copenhagen, you can use this to find people are asking about a pizza place for lunch. Answer your competitors' customer questions and see if you can get them to switch to your company.

Use Twitter to Research

Find out about stuff such as:

- Airlines, flights, cruise ships, hotels, vacation destinations

- Schedules and changes for trains and airplanes

- Movies

- Weekend events

- Nightclubs

- Restaurants

- Doctors, dentists, lawyers, and other local services

- Products and recalls

- Classes

You can also use Twitter to buy or sell stuff. For example, look for cheap gasoline near your zip code. You don't need to use the Advanced Search. In the regular Twitter search box, enter:

"cheap gas" near:"94306" within:5mi

At home, before we make any major purchases, we check Twitter to see what others say. Remember that vendors may add fake tweets, so look at a person's message history to make sure it's honest.

Use Twitter to Find a Job

You can also look for a job. Many companies and job boards post jobs to Twitter because if they can find you directly, they don't have to pay 30% of your salary to a recruiter.

For example, to find jobs in nursing within 20 miles of Atlanta or jobs in banking in Paris, search in Twitter for:

"nursing" "job" near:"30301" within:20mi

intern OR job AND bank near:paris within:50mi since:2018-09-22

You can also use Twitter to find people inside a company and talk with them. Learn the inside story about a job before you join.

Be Findable in Twitter

Make sure people can find you in Twitter. Use the Twitter search box and look for your name, your product, or your organization.

You should also make sure you show up in FollowerWonk.com.

To make it easier to be found, use keywords and hashtags in your profile description (see how I did this at @andreas_ramos) and write tweets with relevant hashtags.

Twitter and SEO

Twitter is a good way to get your web page into Google. If you have a new website, a new page in your website, or you want something to show up in Google, tweet about it. Put a link from your tweet to the page and Google will index the page. Google picks it up almost immediately. When people search for it in Google, your tweet will show up.

Use Google and Bing to see if they can find your tweets and organization in Twitter. For example, if you work for Godiva, search for:

site:twitter.com "godiva chocolate"

This finds the phrase "godiva chocolate" in Twitter.

Closing Summary

Try the different search tools to see how they work.

Chapter 7: Advertising in Twitter

In 2013, Twitter rolled out their advertising platform, cleverly called *Twitter Advertising*. It lets you use keywords and hashtags to write tweets. Twitter shows your tweets to people also who use those hashtags or keywords. You can also limit the tweets to countries, states, or cities. This lets you show your tweet only in Chicago.

This section is for anyone who wants to advertise in Twitter. If you're not using advertising, you can skip this section.

Behavior Targeting in Twitter

Twitter uses demographic targeting. It collects data about a person's behavior (settings, location, your tweets, clicks, searches, and so on). This may also include webpages that she has visited that have Twitter buttons (even if she didn't click anything, Twitter knows she visited the page). This profile of her interests and activities is her *Interest Graph*. Twitter uses this to show your advertising at her.

Set Up and Use Ads

Log into your Twitter account, click your profile icon (at the upper right) and select **Twitter Ads**.

You can promote tweets or write new tweets as ads.

You can also use images and video in Twitter ads. You can use text, photos, or video in a Twitter Card.

Here's an example of a Twitter Card that I made:

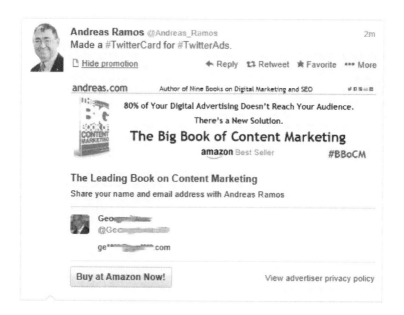

Figure 29: **Twitter Card**. When people click these, their email address is added to your database.

You can also add a call-to-action and URL (such as "Buy at Amazon Now!" and the URL for the book at Amazon.)

The card allows one-click subscription to your newsletter or marketing database. Your visitor clicks the ad and her email address (that she uses at Twitter) is automatically added to your database. You can also download these email addresses from Twitter Advertising. The card tells the user that his name will be shared if he clicks the button.

There are additional options and settings. See the documentation at Twitter.

More about Twitter Cards at dev.twitter.com/cards

How to Track the Results

You can track metrics with Google Analytics' conversion tracking tags.

You Gotta Use It

I like Twitter Ads. It's easy and quick. You can be up in minutes on Twitter.

Chapter 8: Analytics in Twitter

There is a basic analytics report in Twitter.

To use Twitter Analytics, click your small profile icon at the upper right of Twitter. From the drop-down menu, select Analytics. You can also go to analytics.twitter.com/user/YOUR-USER-ID/home (and put your user ID in that URL).

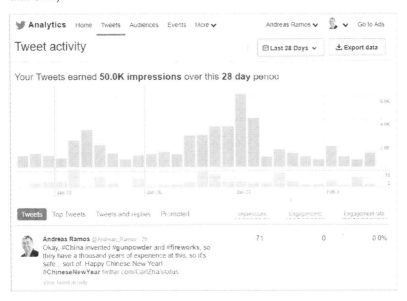

Figure 30: Twitter analytics shows you data and trends for the last 28 days in your account.

Figure 31: You can see trends and numbers for engagement, likes, clicks, replies, and retweets.

Figure 32: Twitter Analytics also shows data about your audience. Okay, my audience (not yours). My followers are really interested in tech, dogs, and science. Should I post more about cyber dogs in space? :-)

There are more screens; I chose a few to show you what is possible.

Closing Summary

This is very basic analytics. It only shows the last 28 days. It would be better to see at least five years of data.

For better data, use Google Analytics.

Chapter 9: Twitter after Dark

There is also the underside of Twitter. I don't include this to encourage you to do these things. Don't. Really. Some of these things are dangerous. The point is to show you the many ways that people use Twitter.

The Underside of Twitter?

You've probably heard about Anthony Weiner, some New York politician, who was posting photos of himself. For whatever reason, some guys post photos of their erections under the hashtag #dickpic. This is remarkably widespread (1,300 in the last thirty days). It's not just guys. Women also post photos of their breasts under #titpic, along with other body parts. Some of these have 950,000 tweets in the last 30 days (over 1,300 tweets per hour). These often include videos.

Facebook won't even allow a photo of a mother nursing her own baby. On Twitter, everything goes.

As you know by now, many teens are active on Twitter. Some 14- and 15-year old girls are posting nude photos of themselves for their boyfriends. This started when fake celebrities released sex tapes to build notoriety.

I was talking with the CEO and CTO of a major social media company. I said, "have you guys seen what some of these teenage girls are up to?" They looked at the floor and said, "Yeah... the moms call us."

Despite the scare stories in the popular media, only 4% of US teens (about 1.2m) post dumb things, according to the Pew study. 96% of teens don't cause problems.

Hookers use Twitter to offer services. They post with #callgirl, #escort, #rentboy, along with a zip code, such as 10005 (for Wall Street) or 20003 (the US Congress in Washington D.C). Customers find them by searching for hashtags and zip codes. See? It's not followers. It's hashtags that matter.

People will tweet to buy drugs, offer drugs, or brag about drugs they just bought. They don't realize their postings can be seen by the whole world, including the police. Cops, even in small towns, have learned how to use social media to watch for hashtags such as #meth, #molly, and so on.

Street gangs often send out tweets to brag about their crimes. These often include photos and videos of themselves in the act. "Woohoo! We robbed the corner store! Here's pix of us with the money!" Police click "Like" on those.

I write about these things to show you what's going on in Twitter. Practically none of my friends who work in social media in Silicon Valley knew about these things.

The People Are in the Tweets!

There's been a great deal of talk about the role of social media in the color revolutions, such as the Orange Revolution in the Ukraine, the Rose Revolution in Georgia, the Green Revolution in Iran, along with the Jasmine Revolution in Tunisia and the Arab Spring (Egypt, Bahrain, and other countries). There have also been riots in London, Paris, and Stockholm.

However, closer study shows the role of social media in the Arab revolts has been minor. Only 1% of Egyptians have access to Twitter. It's not social that causes revolts. Repressive and corrupt regimes increase social tension. Governments give preference to the extremely wealthy and show indifference towards youths. TV and popular culture glamorize the wealthy.

There's high unemployment among teens worldwide. US teen unemployment is 24% which is triple the adult rate. 30% of Americans in their 20s live at home. The numbers are worse in the UK, Spain, Italy, and Greece. This is a recipe for trouble.

Teens use Twitter to talk with each other and this is mostly invisible to adults. Instead of doing anything to improve social problems, the British government has threatened to shut off Twitter, SMS, and cell phones. If governments prevent discussion, that increases distrust, miscommunication, and tension.

Bjørn Bredal wrote in *Politiken* that activists in Egypt and Palestine agreed social media allowed the public to develop opinions that weren't censored by the state-controlled media. Protesters could organize quickly and share information. However, after the governments were overthrown, social media was not useful. The people had to create new governments and social structures, but social media turned conversation into endless comments and myriad opinions which were impossible to bring together to a common goal. The Arab activists said the old media was better when it served as a public service to present trusted information.

Indeed, we've seen the same in the US. Despite fifteen years of social media platforms, political groups and activists haven't been able to use it to organize movements in a meaningful or long-lasting way.

Political Harassment and Censorship

While writing this book, I talked with engineers who worked for companies that create fake accounts. These companies work for other companies or governments. They use these accounts as sock puppets to either create fake support or attack critics.

A well-known example happened during the Russian Parliament elections in December 2011. There was massive election fraud by the governing political party, both in suppressing valid votes and adding fake votes. Voters and observers discussed the fraud on Twitter. Over 500,000 messages were sent.

In retaliation, 25,860 fake accounts sent 440,793 fake tweets at 1,846 tweets per minute. They flooded the conversation to prevent discussion. The fake Tweets included hashtags, jeering, and nonsense text. A prominent Russian anti-corruption blogger was attacked by 4,215 fake accounts.

26,000 sybil accounts were connected as a sybil network. This shows a single organization was behind the attack. (Sybil accounts are named after Sybil, a famous case of a person with multiple personality disorder.)

While writing this, I wondered if there was sybil harassment in the US. If you look at magazines or newspapers generally considered to be progressive or liberal (in the American sense of the word), the comments section is often filled with spam, rabid attacks, or ridicule. I've often wondered why an extreme rightist would read the *New York Review of Books* or similar magazines.

So I looked at *Fox News* (a right-wing TV station in the US). Oddly enough, the few comments are generally people who applauded the news items or called for even stricter positions. I spent an hour and found no attacks or ridicule from the opposition. It may be there, but it isn't as widespread as on the other side.

Journalists have written about services that carry out hacking, smearing, and content spamming on competitors, journalists, and political activists on behalf of companies.

How to Bypass Censors

If your government is trying to shut off web communications, you can post to Twitter (but you can't receive) by sending a tweet to:

- UK: +447624800379

- GERMANY: +491724403473

- FINLAND: +3584573950042

These are international SMS messages. Careful. International SMS messages can be $0.25 to $0.50 (or more).

Create a Twitter Account via SMS

You don't need to have a Twitter account to use it. You can set this up via your phone.

- Send a text message to your Twitter short code (such as 40404 if you're in the US) with the word **START**

- Twitter will ask for your name

- Twitter then sends you a username

- That's all. Start using your account.

- You can change settings by SMS. For more, go to http://bit.ly/J58eeK

If you don't want to be tracked, use a disposable phone and create an account with the phone.

Use Twitter on Dumb Phones

Twitter also works via SMS on basic phones. You can buy a $5 disposable cell phone at any large drugstore or supermarket. (Look for TracFone or similar.) These phones include free minutes to start. You can add more minutes. Connect the cell phone to your account and you can send/receive tweets.

Note: the phones charge by the minute and message. If you buy 10 minutes, you have for example ten minutes of talk or 30 SMS messages.

This is another difference between Twitter and Facebook: you can't use Facebook on a dumb phone.

Privacy and Blackmail

There's no privacy on Twitter. It's easy for companies and governments to figure out who you are by correlating your IP address, your location, and your various social identities. Various governments do this.

If you want to remain private, use an unregistered, throw-away phone. Don't carry your usual phone with you because its location can be tracked, even when it's turned off, and matched to your unregistered phone. Don't write in your normal style.

Sexual Harassment

In the UK, Caroline Criado-Perez successfully petitioned the Bank of England to put a portrait of Jane Austen on the ten pound note. That was a rather nice idea.

Inexplicably, several people began attacking her on Twitter. She received many threats of violence, rape, and murder.

- Don't reply. They want attention.

- Block them. Go to the person's profile. Click the dropdown menu and select "Block."

- Report them to Twitter. Use the "Report Abuse" button. At the end of a tweet, select More | Abusive.

- Contact the police. Give them copies of the tweets. It's a crime to make violent threats.

Some people think there are no rules for online behavior. They use Twitter to send nasty, brutish, short messages. The same social rules and legal limits apply to both public and online behavior.

Figure 33: Don't put up with abusive tweets. Use the **Abuse** button. A team at Twitter will review the tweets and block the user.

Politics and Twitter

Political parties and organizations in many countries have realized they can use (misuse) social media for politics. David Cole (@DavidColeACLU), National Legal Director of the ACLU and a professor at Georgetown, wrote about social media in the New York Review of Books (Feb. 7, 2019). In his review of the book *Twitter and Tear Gas* by Zeynep Tufekci (@zeynep), Cole writes, "The goal is not to shut down opposing views, but to produce resignation, cynicism, and a sense of disempowerment among the people. This can be done in many ways, including inundating audiences with information, producing distractions to dilute their attention and focus, delegitimating media that provide accurate information..., deliberately sowing confusion, fear, and doubt by aggressively questioning credibility,... creating or claiming hoaxes, or generating harassment campaigns."

Trump and Twitter

I suppose I should write something about Twitter's best-known user. When Donald Trump (@RealDonaldTrump) published a book in 2009, a marketing staffer suggested he should use Twitter for publicity. For the first few years, he posted between nine in the morning to six in the evening. In early 2013, he found he could use Twitter to attack Obama and began tweeting pretty much 24 hours a day. After 2016, he tweets from six in the morning to midnight. He has tried several other social media sites, but he prefers Twitter.

Trump uses Twitter to broadcast. He talks at the world. But that's all he does with Twitter; he doesn't use Threads, Lists, or polls. Photos and videos are nearly always taken by someone else. It's a bit odd that Trump uses Twitter. He is 72 years old. Few 70-year olds use social media.

In comparison, Alexandria Ocasio-Cortez (@AOC) with three million followers is the most successful social media user among Democrats. Her tweets nearly always include photographs and videos which she took herself, Her postings are a mix of work and personal tweets. But she also doesn't use Lists or Threads.

Trump has 58 million followers. Statuspeople.com reports 9% are fake, 12% are active, and 79% are inactive, which is about seven million followers with active accounts (@AOC has 21% fake, 40% inactive, and 39% active). However, "active" doesn't mean someone is reading those tweets. It just means the account is active. The Guardian wrote about the interaction rate, which is the number of interactions (comments, retweets, likes) against the number of followers. Alexandria Ocasio-Cortez has a 2.8% interaction rate for the last 90 days (up to Feb 10, 2019). In comparison, Obama's is 0.4%, Hillary Clinton's is 0.2%, Donald Trump's is 0.2%, and Bernie Sanders' is 0.09%. (All of these numbers are easy to fake.)

Trump often announces his decisions and staff firing in tweets, so journalists, politicians, the White House staff, and many governments follow him closely.

You can read more about Trump on Twitter at t2m.io/Pu34EXy7

Summary

When you read this chapter, you may begin to think Twitter is out of control. Porn stars, drug dealers, gangs, rape threats, terrorists, and political extremists are on the loose in Twitter.

For most of recorded history, the elite held complete power over economics, the legal system, the church, and the military. They banned writers, burned books, and imprisoned poets, writers, and scientists.

But social media breaks that control, not by confrontation, but bypassing it. Social makes it possible for anyone to talk with anyone. People can share ideas, plans, and actions.

There is much talk about censorship in China, but in reality, many use VPNs and other tools to bypass censorship. The government tolerates it because it needs the flow of information.

Social media's open communication is both good and bad. It's good that researchers, academics, technical people, and others can share ideas, which leads to progress. It's bad that irresponsible people use social media to harass and attack. Many people are also misinformed and they spread false ideas.

Social media isn't just something for marketing. It's much more than that. Nobody had any idea when Gutenberg invented the printing press in 1440 AD that it would result in revolutions, wars, the collapse of religion, the rise of science, and the modern world. Nearly 600 years later, a new communications revolution is happening with the web, search engines, social media, and mobile devices.

Nobody knows where this will lead.

Chapter 10: Police on Twitter

I also noticed the police are active on Twitter so I met with the Palo Alto Police and Mountain View Police to talk about Twitter and social media.

There are almost 18,000 police departments in the US. Several thousand use social media for investigation and outreach. They do investigation, of course, but community policing outreach is more important: they see social media as a way to improve transparency. It allows the police to have a personal presence and collaborate with the community. They can reach out to the public and the public can also contact them.

The Boston Marathon Bombing was a watershed moment because it was the first time the public could get accurate information in a major crisis directly from the police. In the general panic after the bombing, the web was filled with rumors. The Boston police used Twitter to update people about the search for suspects. When the suspect was finally surrounded and captured, the police tweeted updates every few minutes. This raised the bar for police agencies.

Social also allows the police to bypass the news media and reach the public directly. Newspapers and TV/radio news often spin stories to make them more dramatic, which attracts viewers, which increases advertising revenues. Crime in the US has fallen steadily for more than 30 years to record lows, but you won't know that if you watch TV news in the US.

When the police told the media that they were going to start using social, the news media said please, don't do that, it takes the news away from us.

Previously, the police held press conferences. While police still hold press conferences, they now post directly to social media. This gives them their own broadcast capability. The result is greater accuracy because the news media can't spin the story. Instead, the media now often retweet the police tweets, which increases the police's outreach.

Here's an example. Several years ago, two Palo Alto police officers stopped a car on a busy downtown street at lunchtime. The driver raced away, crashing into several cars and then fled on foot. The cops ran after him for a few blocks. People in cafes and restaurants began tweeting about police car chases, hostages, guns, and so on. The police replied immediately in Twitter that none of that was happening. It was just a foot chase. They can clarify, correct, and update, which calms the situation and prevents the spread of public misinformation.

Social also allows police to be seen as human. Some of the tweets are really funny. One day, they tweeted they would set up a speed trap at an intersection. After they caught one guy, they tweeted he should have been following the cop's tweets.

You can follow them at @PaloAltoPolice and @MountainViewPD

They also use YouTube for videos and Pinterest to post photos of lost and found items, their police dogs, the officers, and other items (go to pinterest.com/mountainviewpd/boards/). Both Palo Alto and Mountain View police are also using NextDoor, a social media site that's based on neighborhoods.

In the San Francisco Bay Area, over 50 departments, including police, fire, ambulance, and other emergency groups share information through the Bay Area Law Enforcement Social Media Group (#BALESMG). Other cities can contact them to learn more.

There's also IACPSocialMedia, a central resource for social media for the police. Many of their FAQs and presentations can be used by your organization for your social media strategies.

Several companies offer social media software for the police. These allow police to monitor tweets within their community. They can mark off an area on a map, select terms such as #cocaine or #shooting, and get alerts when these words show up in tweets within their cities. The police can also add a list of users to monitor. The software shows the tweet, the type of device that was used to post the tweet, and if it's enabled on the device, the GPS location. By clicking on the user, the police can see the person's past tweets, posted pictures, and tweet habits. The police can download the most recent 10,000 tweets that match the users, keywords and place names in their watch list. If they're following someone and the person tweets, there's an alert beep and if GPS is enabled on the device, a dot shows up on the map. The police can zoom down to street view to see the location.

Summary

There's good and bad about the police on social media. The police in Palo Alto in Silicon Valley use it to talk with the community and keep an eye on criminals. However, in other cities or countries, the police use it to monitor legitimate dissidents and critics, which isn't good.

Chapter 11: Twitter in Disasters

Many people think Twitter will be good for information during disasters such as earthquakes, hurricanes, and giant monsters marching out of the ocean.

One of my neighbors is a geologist for the USGS, the US government office that monitors earthquakes. We live in Palo Alto, just a few miles from the San Andreas Fault, where California earthquakes happen.

He told me that in a serious earthquake (or any major regional disaster), too many people will be making phone calls, which will overwhelm calls to and between ambulance, hospitals, fire, and other emergency services. The authorities will shut down the telephone system. Only calls to emergencies services will work.

This also means the Internet and the web may be shut off. This means no Twitter via the web.

If a major disaster happens, you *should* be able to use your cell phone SMS (instant messaging) because SMS uses the text messaging system, which doesn't take up much bandwidth.

So learn how to use SMS and be able to contact someone outside of your region.

You'll notice I wrote, "you *should* be able." In theory, this should work, but nobody knows, because this has never happened. Furthermore, Twitter.com is in San Francisco, where a major earthquake is likely. Twitter admits in their S-1 SEC document (p. 51, Oct. 4th, 2013) that their data isn't distributed across data centers, so if (which means, when) an earthquake happens, it's not clear when Twitter will be up again or whether they'll even have a building.

To Use Twitter with SMS

You can link your cell phone's SMS text messaging to Twitter.

- First, link your Twitter account to your phone. Go to your Twitter account. Click Settings | Mobile. Enter your phone number. Twitter will send you a confirmation code.

- Use your phone to send to the Twitter Short Code. For example, in the US, post to Twitter by sending SMS to **40404**. Get a list of the SMS short codes for every country at support.twitter.com/articles/20170024.

- To turn on all tweets (everyone you follow), send "**ON**" (Be careful! If you follow 500 people, your phone may explode.)

- To turn off all tweets, send **OFF**

- To follow (or add) someone, send "**ON**" and the name, e.g., **ON ANDREAS_RAMOS** (you can use lower case)

- To stop following someone, send "**OFF**" and the name, e.g., **OFF ANDREAS_RAMOS**

- To get help, send **HELP**

- More commands at support.twitter.com/sms

Try this on your phone. Learn how to do this.

You can also go to Twitter.com to set up who you want to follow on your cell phone. Look at the list of people you follow. Next to the blue Following button, click the down arrow and select Turn On Mobile Notifications. You'll get her tweets on your phone via SMS.

Twitter Alerts

Twitter has partnered with over 100 emergency services to allow them to send tweets with alerts and information during emergencies.

Summary

When you really need this chapter, it won't be the time to start to learn. Go ahead and try Twitter with SMS.

Examples of Using Twitter

Here are several ways you can use Twitter to promote a theater production or your participation in a conference. You can adapt this for talking about your organization, services, or products.

Use Twitter to Promote a Theater Play

(A friend is an actor in San Francisco. I wrote the following to help them promote their plays. I changed a few names. You can use these ideas to promote any kind of event.)

So you want to promote a theater performance. It doesn't matter if your only follower is your cat. Take these steps to reach your audience.

Use a unique hashtag for the play. The play is *Feng Niao* in San Francisco (SF), so use #FengNiaoSF.

- Everyone (actors, stage crew, support, friends, family, dogs, and so on) should set up Twitter accounts.

- Everyone should post DAILY to their Twitter accounts. If someone posts two or three times daily, even better. Use the hashtag #FengNiaoSF in every tweet.

- Put #FengNiaoSF (with the pound/hash) on the play's webpage so it can be found by Google/Bing

- Post the following in Twitter and Facebook: "See FengNiao Theater in #SF #FortMason, Sept. 13-23. Go http://bit.ly/15ZR1ON #FengNiaoSF. Please Retweet!" That places the hashtag, city, and the link to the event. The bit.ly/15ZR1ON is a compressed URL for your event. Click it and you'll see it goes to your site.

- Add tweets with information about the play, such as "FengNiao by Qian Zhongshu," "#FengNiaoSF directed by @StephanieACota," "FengNiao at SF #FortMason Theater," "See @WendyLChang in #FengNiaoSF." Include names of cast, backstage, and so on.

- The play is about Chinese in San Francisco. Add hashtags tweets to reach the Chinese community, such as #China #Beijing #Shanghai, and so on.

- Each person in the play should tweet his/her personal experiences each day. The more personal, the better.

- Don't just send text. Add photos and video clips.

- Send backstage photos, funny videos, rehearsals, outtakes, and goofs. Send photos and videos of the cast and audience, the cast with kids, the cast with dogs, the cast after a night.

- Do call-and-response among your cast. One person tweets #IfFengNiaoWasYourMom (one word with hashtag) and others respond with flippant, creative, or thoughtful responses, such as #IfFengNiaoWasYourMom she'd put sugar in your baby bottle.

- Use Hootsuite to set up a search stream for #FengNiaoSF so you can follow the postings.

- Interview people. What's your favorite line? Who's your favorite character?

- Do video interviews with audience. Roaming cell phone camera and pick someone out in the line and ask questions. What do you expect to see tonight? How did you hear about this? Afterwards: What did you think of the play? What did you think of her?

- Set up Twitter advertising. The ads can start a few weeks before the play and end with the play. You can set the ads to show only in San Francisco.

And of course, send tweets such as:

- #DateNightIdeas: go to #FengNiaoSF

- #MondayNightSF: go to #FengNiaoSF

- #TuesdayNightSF: go to #FengNiaoSF

- #SF #Events: go to #FengNiaoSF

- #WhatToDo Sept SF: Go to #FengNiaoSF

- #ShootYourTV. Go to #FengNiaoSF

- #CheatOnYourWife. Take your girlfriend to #FengNiaoSF.

- #CheatOnYourGirlfriend. Take your wife to #FengNiaoSF.

- Look for current events in San Francisco and connect them to FengNiao. When people look for those events, they'll see your tweets. Here are examples:

- Giant #SeaMonster knocked #GoldenGateBridge down yet again? Go to #FengNiaoSF

- Warning, commuters! Giant #SeaMonster ate #GoldenGateBridge. Until fixed, go to #FengNiaoSF

- #BusStrike? Go to #FengNiaoSF

- Skip the #Giants! Go to #FengNiaoSF

- No tickets for #MileyCyrus? Go to #FengNiaoSF

- Line too long for #TomCruise movie? Go to #FengNiaoSF

- #Tourist in #SF? Go to #FengNiaoSF

- Who cares about #OracleWorld! Go to #FengNiaoSF

- What do locals do in #SF? Go to #FengNiaoSF

- No more #hookers in #Tenderloin? Go to #FengNiaoSF

- OMFG! Extreme #Theater at #FengNiaoSF

- #BayArea #theater at #FengNiaoSF

- #Oakland #theater at #FengNiaoSF

See? Maybe only your cat is following you on Twitter, but you can reach your audience.

Use Twitter at a Conference

You can use Twitter to create awareness and make contacts at a conference. Here's a plan that I wrote for a conference in NYC.

- Every employee in your team should set up a Twitter account. You want to create a large digital presence.

- Set this up on your cell phones and practice before you go to NYC.

- Each person should tweet at least once a day, and perhaps 2-3 times per day. One or two people also post to the company's Twitter account.

- Learn how to send tweets that include text, hashtags, shortened URLs, photos, and video.

- Have contests. Who sent the MOST tweets in 24 hours with the company hashtag? Win ice cream. Who got the most retweets for one message during the conference week? The CEO will sing to you at dinner. Who sent the best photo? Who sent a photo that got the most retweets? Who sent a video that got the most retweets?

- Do video interviews. Ask conference attendees, "Why are you here?" "How did you hear about this?" Ask unexpected questions such as "What's your suggestion for the CEO of Google?"

- Use Google Analytics on your website to track data to see the impact.

- Add Hootsuite on your phone or tablet and set up a search stream for your company hashtag so you can follow the postings.

- You can write tweets in Hootsuite before you go to NYC to be posted while you're in NYC.

- Ask people questions at the conference. "What did you think of the last presentation?" "We're going out for dinner, join us."

- Set up Twitter advertising to shows your top tweets to your audience. The ads can start and stop with the conference. You can also set the ads to show only in New York City. Everyone at the conference will see your tweets.

Here are ideas for tweets:

- When you attend speaking events or meetings, tweet the top ideas.

- Invite people to meeting: For example, "Meet #EzyInsights in #NYC @EzyInsights."

- Write tweets in the languages that people use at the conference: English, Chinese, German, French, Spanish, and so on

- Post your personal experiences for the day. @EzyInsights going to #EmpireStateBuilding

- Don't be formal. Send funny photos of the team. The team at a bar. The CEO with hookers. The CEO getting arrested by NY police.

- Use photos and video.

Use the event's hashtag, such as #AdWeekNYC, to tweet points by speakers, event information, or find people to share taxi, cultural outings, dinners, or shuttle to the airport.

Sometimes, conference organizers haven't set up a hashtag for the event. You should take the opportunity to create the hashtag.

- Create an acronym hashtag. For Advertising Week Los Angeles in 2014, try #AdWeekLA14. Conference organizers can use hashtags for cities and years, such as AdWeekLA13, AdWeekUK13, AdWeekLA14, and so on.

- Make sure the hashtag looks okay (and makes sense) in lower case. #adweekla14 is okay. #PenIsland would be regrettable.

- See if anyone else is using the hashtag. Search for it in Twitter. Sometimes, it was in use a year ago, but no longer, and that's okay. You don't want a hashtag that someone else is currently using.

- When you've come up with a good hashtag, send an email to the conference organizers and suggest the hashtag. Ask them to include it in their website and emails.

- Start using it. Post three or four tweets about the conference, such as #UKFOLS13 (Family Office Leadership Summit in London, 2013).

- Because you came up with it, you own the hashtag. Post before, during, and after the event.

Strategy for a Twitter Project

Here are several steps to manage Twitter account for a company:

- Find five to ten competitors of the same size and market. These should be companies that are not too small or too large. They should be in the same general market and country as your company. You should also look at companies in the US; they often have good Twitter accounts. Follow those Twitter accounts. Review the accounts carefully. What are they doing well? What are they doing poorly? Which ideas can you borrow? Write a one-to-two page summary of each account. Update this every quarter. (Tip: so your competitors don't know that you're following them, create an extra Twitter account and use it to follow them).

- Do keyword research to find the top keywords and hashtags for the company and its products. Create a list and share with your team.

- Set up Twitter management tools (Hootsuite and TweetDeck). Use these to track the competitors and top keywords. Use these to schedule postings to the account. If you have a team, set them up so their draft tweets go to you for review and approval.

- Set up Google Analytics (or whichever web analytics that your company uses) to track the Twitter traffic

- Make written suggestions to improve the Twitter account

- Plan and set up a calendar of events, product releases, and so on, including holidays, company events, and other public events. Use the calendar to plan your postings for twelve months. Share this with your team.

- Post tweets that use keywords, photos, videos with pinned tweets, polls, threaded tweets, moments, and so on

- Get your audience to react. Ask open questions. Reply to comments from your audience.

- Post to the competitors' accounts so their followers become aware of your company

- Find the top people in your industry. Follow them. Reply to their postings.

- Urge people in your company to join Twitter. Set up training so they begin to use Twitter.

- Every month, write a one-page report on activities, results, data, and plans

More Ideas for Using Twitter

Here's another example. Groupon (an online coupon site in the US) asked their followers "What restaurants would you like coupons for?" Lots of people made suggestions of restaurants (and other kinds of businesses), which allowed Groupon to show restaurants that there was actual demand for coupons. This led to the highest engagement that Groupon ever had. The idea is simple: just ask your customers what they want.

Have you seen great uses of Twitter? Have you come up with clever ideas? Have you used Twitter for your products, company, school, church, and so on? Write a one- or two-page summary and send it to me, and I'll post it to the webpage for this book.

In Closing: So Why Twitter?

You can see by now what Twitter is about. People use Twitter for several reasons:

- Broadcast: Celebrities, movie stars, sport athletes, musicians, artists, key business people, politicians, and marketers use Twitter to broadcast to their followers. It's free to reach them.

- Discussion: Everyone else uses Twitter to talk together. Journalists use it to hear from people and do research for news articles. People talk with others in their professions, jobs, interests, and hobbies. People look for jobs or research before they buy. Police talk with their town. Teens talk together. Use hashtags to find these conversations.

On Twitter, any tweet can be seen by anyone. You can see what anyone is saying. You can follow any topic. You can contact anyone. You can follow them, you can send messages to them, and you can talk with them. Twitter is easy to use because it's microblogging for mobile devices.

Andreas Ramos
Palo Alto, California
February 2019

Resources

Your Ideas, Suggestions, and Changes

Is there something I should add? Do you know of a clever or interesting use of Twitter? Let me know. Send me an email.

My Newsletter

Sign up for my newsletter so I can let you know when there's an updated version or new books. Subscribe at https://eepurl.com/wC-C1

Webpage for this Book

The page for this book is at andreas.com/book-twitterbook.html

Contact Andreas

Questions? Just ask.

- Website: andreas.com
- Twitter: @andreas_ramos
- This book andreas.com/book-twitterbook.html

Articles, Research, and Sources

Links to these articles and research papers are at the webpage for this book.

- *Adapting Social Spam Infrastructure for Political Censorship* by Kurt Thomas, Chris Grier, and Vern Paxson. Details on the spam attack over the Russian Parliament elections. Proceedings of the USENIX Workshop on Large-Scale Exploits and Emergent Threats (LEET). http://bit.ly/1agENDU

- *Hatching Twitter: A True Story of Money, Power, Friendship, and Betrayal* by Nick Bolton (Portfolio Hardcover, November, 2013). The inside story of how Twitter was created. Backstabbing, lies, and betrayal. Excerpt at http://nyti.ms/15kLBlr

- *Intrinsic versus Image-Related Motivations in Social Media* by Prof. Olivier Toubia, Columbia Business School, and Prof. Andrew Stephen, University of Pittsburgh (PDF). How do people behave on Twitter? The researchers picked 2,500 random users and added 100 fake followers to some of these users to see the impact. When people have only a few followers, their postings are generally personal. As the number of followers increases, people began to post more often, but they also begin to broadcast. Postings become less personal. When they reached a certain number of followers, people actually began to post less. The researchers argue there are two reasons for using social: *intrinsic* (by which the researchers mean "for its own sake") and *image* (which means "to enhance status"). To put it bluntly: people either post for fun ("Woohoo! Party!") or to brag ("Dinner at the Four Seasons!").

- *Kan Facebook og Twitter redde 'foråret'?* ("Can Facebook and Twitter Save the Arab Spring?") by Bjørn Bredal (Politiken, Sept. 16, 2013, in Danish. Regrettably, the article is no longer online) .

- *Linked: The New Science of Networks* by Albert-Laszlo Barabasi (Plume, 2003). The theory of networks shows that networks (social networks, websites, the biological food chain, business and commerce, the growth of cities, intra-cellular proteins, and so on) share the same properties, which means they can be quantified and described with mathematical laws. Summary of the book at andreas.com/faq-barabasi.html

- *Trial by Twitter* by Ariel Levy (*The New Yorker*, August 5, 2013). This article led me to realize that non-marketing people were using Twitter in new ways. http://nyr.kr/13jrH64

- *Teens, Social Media, and Privacy* by Mary Madden et al (May 21, 2013). Research by The Pew Research Center for the Pew Internet & American Life Project. They study how people use the Internet and the web. This document covers their research on how teens use social media. http://bit.ly/191zI4W

If you find interesting or useful research on Twitter, please let me know.

More Books from Andreas

You can find more useful stuff in my other books. Go to andreas.com/books.html

Glossary

- **@mention:** An @mention is a tweet that includes an @ within the tweet, such as "Having lunch tomorrow @Laura in Palo Alto." Everyone in Twitter can see your message. See also *@reply*.

- **@reply:** An @reply is a tweet that starts with an @, such as "@Laura, how about lunch?" Your followers and her followers can see the tweet, but not the rest of the world. See also *@mention*.

- **40404:** The SMS code for Twitter in the US and many countries. Send an SMS to 40404 and it will be sent as a tweet. You must have your account connected to your cell phone number. Get a list of the SMS short codes for every country at support.twitter.com/articles/20170024.

- **Direct Message (DM):** By starting a tweet with DM and a user's name, you can send a direct message (DM) to her. For example, "DM @Laura Can we move lunch to Tuesday?" Only Laura will see the message. To be able to send her a message, she has to be following you. She can also change her settings so anyone can send her a direct message.

- **Followers:** People who subscribe to your tweets. It doesn't really matter since most won't ever see your tweets. Hashtags are more important.

- **Hashtags:** Add a hashmark (#) to a word to mark it as a special word, just like underlining or using bold to mark a word. People use hashtags so they can follow tweets about a topic. This turns tweets into a conversation. For example, #Apple is the hashtag for Apple computers, so when people want to know 1about Apple, they search for #Apple. Read the chapter on hashtags to learn more, including tools for discovering and following hashtags.

- **Interest Graph:** Twitter collects data on your activity: how you describe yourself in your profile (keywords, location, and so on), who you follow, who follows you, what you click, what you search, and so on. This builds up your Interest Graph, a picture of what you do. Advertisers can use this to select audiences. See also Facebook's *Social Graph* (the map of a person's social connections) and Google's *Knowledge Graph* (the map of information).

- **Social media**: Social media platforms such as Twitter and Facebook allow group communication, sharing, editing, collaboration, and other activities. Social media platforms lack tools for collaboration, sharing, editing, storage, and so on. Some day, someone will build a better social media platform.

- **Sock Puppets:** Some people use fake accounts to either cheer what they said themselves ("Hey, that's a great idea!) or attack themselves. It's like they're talking with a sock puppet. They also use fake accounts to attack other people so it appears many are against the person. In some cases, this can be thousands of fake accounts. See also *Sybil accounts*.

- **Sybil Accounts:** Another name for sock puppets. These are fake accounts. This is named after Sybil, a famous psychiatric case of a person with multiple-personality disorder. See also *sock puppets*.

- **Sybil Network:** When hundreds of fake accounts are linked together to appear as a group, it's a fake group. See also *sybil* accounts and *sock puppets*.

Index

#FF Follow Friday, 21

#MileyCyrus, 25

@mention, 38

@reply, 38

40404 and Twitter, 82

Add Twitter to webpage, 14

Advanced Search, 62

Analytics, 67

Austen, Jane, 74

Bird, Larry, 8

Bjørn, Bredal, 91

Black teens on Twitter, 52

Black Twitter, 54

Block people, 40

Book's webpage, 90

Bredal, Bjørn, 72

Buy fake followers, 20

Cat
  Caturday, 21
  Fake account, 21
  Follower, 18, 83, 85
  House cat, 2
  Twitter account, 21
Cell phone, 11, 82

Censors, 73

Change the background, 9

China, 56

Clark, Monte, 2

Clicky-clicky, 20

Contact Andreas, 90

Create fake followers, 20

Criado-Perez, Caroline, 74

Crime on Twitter, 71

Dashboards, 40

Direct Message
  DM, 39
  Notifications, 11
  Private messages, 39
DisplayPurposes.com, 27

DM message, 39

Dog
  Company mascot, 59
Dogs
  In Space, 69
  Lunch again, 26
  Police, 79
  Yet again, 83
  Your profile photo, 9
Dot before the @mention, 38

Download your tweets, 42

Dumb phones and Twitter, 74

Earthquakes, 81

Engagement, 58

Facebook
  Backyard party, 6
  Compared with Twitter, 6
  Hashtags, 24, 31
  Teen users, 51
Fake accounts, 60

Find a job, 64

Findable in Twitter, 64

Follow Friday, 21

Followers, 17

FollowerWonk, 18

Free photos, 31

Glossary, 93

Granovetter, Mark, 26

Hashtagify.me, 29

Hashtags

> At Google and Facebook, 24
> Copyright, 25
> Hijacking, 39
> Ignored by Twitter, 24
> Origins, 24
> Ownership, 25
> Tools for hashtags, 27
> Trademark, 25
> What are they?, 24

Hookers on Twitter, 70

Hootsuite, 41

How to write a tweet, 30

Hsiung, Chris, 2

Hurricanes, 81

IRC chat groups, 24

Isaac, Mike, 60

Kardashian, Kim, 17

Latino teens on Twitter, 52

Lists in Twitter, 43

Moments, 34

Monsters attacking, 81

Multiple accounts, 12

Mute people, 40

Namgostar, Ginger, 2

New Yorker, 5

Number of users, 59

Perron, Zach, 2

Pew study, 51, 60, 92

Pin a tweet, 32

Police, 78

Polls, 31

Privacy on Twitter, 74

Private accounts, 11

Pulse of the Tweeters, 28

Recover access, 13

References, 91

Research with Twitter, 63

Retweet, 35

Revolutions, 71

RiteTag, 28

RT, 35

Russian Parliment, 72

Sea monster attacks, 85

Search box in Twitter, 62

SEO and Twitter, 64

Set up Twitter, 9

SMS and Twitter, 81

Social media, 94

Sock puppets, 72

Steubenville, 5

Take over an ID, 13

Teens on Twitter, 51

Threads, 33

TrendsMap, 29

Trump, Donald, 76

Tweet cloud, 38

Tweetchat, 36

Tweetdesk, 41

Tweets, Tips, 35

Twitter

> Advertising, 65

Bird, 8
Black teens, 54
Chaos, 6
Different uses, 7
Disasters, 81
Egyptian revolution, 6
For business, 58
Latinos, 55
Origins, 6
Police, 78
Promote a conference, 85
Promote a play, 83
Revolutions, 71
S-1 SEC document, 81
Set up, 9
SMS code, 82

Teen users, 51
TV, 57
What is it?, 7
Your ID, 10
Twitter Alerts, 82

Twitter Card, 65

Verified Accounts, 12

Webpage for the book, 90

WeChat, 56

Who to follow, 18

Word cloud, 37

More Books by Andreas

Startup
by Andreas Ramos
amazon #1 Best Seller

How to build your Silicon Valley startup, find co-founders, deal with investors, and sell your startup. Interviews with 26 founders, accelerators, and VCs.

Get the #1 Amazon Best Seller in English, French, Korean, Spanish, and Chinese. Available worldwide. See andreas.com

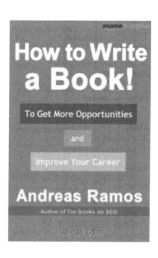

How to Write a Book!
By Andreas Ramos
amazon #1 Best Seller

Why write a book? A book brings you opportunities: speaking engagements, projects, jobs, invitations to join advisory boards with pre-IPO stock, and invitations to start companies. Learn how to write and publish your book in 90 days.

Go to andreas.com

#TwitterBook by @Andreas_Ramos

Notes

Notes

Printed in Poland
by Amazon Fulfillment
Poland Sp. z o.o., Wrocław